I love you,
May God bless
you and keep you
always,
Jennifer Wake

MW00619867

Dear Salena,
Love & miss
you very much!
Shellie

Salena/Army!
So glad we've
crossed paths!
I love that
I see you
in COS!
love you!
Go Navy!!!
KG

FREE TO BE BRAVE

Moments with God for Military Life

Love and
miss you!
Ginger

Love you
so much
girl!
Claudia

Bless you
my sparkly
friend! Love + miss you
Brenda

Because we love you!
Living for Real
Lou

From the *Planting Roots* Community

Compiled by Ginger Harrington

Edited by Ginger Harrington, Katye Riselli, and Liz Giertz

Many blessings sweet Salena!
Miss you and your beautiful smile. Katie

Published by Planting Roots Corporation, P.O. Box 84, Leavenworth, Kansas 66048

Cover photo by Rachael Jernigan.
Cover design by Ginger Harrington and Liz Giertz
Compiled by Ginger Harrington
Edited by Ginger Harrington, Katye Riselli, and Liz Giertz

Planting Roots is a nonprofit organization encouraging military women to grow in their faith.

This is dedicated to the women who serve our nation in the military community: women in uniform, wives, moms, and daughters. May these words encourage you and strengthen you so you may thrive wherever your military journey leads.

<u>Enjoy the companion Bible study from Planting Roots</u>

Free to Be Brave: Moments with God for Military Life
CreateSpace Independent Publishing Platform (November 2018)

<u>Other Books from Authors on the Planting Roots Staff</u>

Holy in the Moment: Simple Ways to Love God and Enjoy Your Life
Ginger Harrington, Abingdon Press (2018)

Journey of a Military Wife Series
Brenda Pace, American Bible Society (2017):
Directed: Steps of Peace
Deployed: Steps of Hope
Devoted: Steps of Love
Dedicated: Steps of Faith

Medals Above My Heart: The Rewards of Being a Military Wife
Brenda Pace and Carol McGlothlin, B & H Books, 2004

The One Year Yellow Ribbon Devotional:
Take a Stand in Prayer for Our Nation and Those Who Serve
Brenda Pace and Carol McGlothlin, Tyndale House Publishers, (2008)

Olive Drab Pom-Poms
Kori Yates, Crossbooks, (2011)

Marriage Maintenance for Her: Tune Up After Time Apart
Liz Giertz, CreateSpace Independent Publishing Platform (2018)

Marriage Maintenance for Him: Tune Up After Time Apart
Liz Giertz, CreateSpace Independent Publishing Platform (2018)

When Marriage Gets Messy: Overcoming 10 Common Messes Married Couples Make
Liz Giertz, CreateSpace Independent Publishing Platform (2018)

Discipleship 101
Andrea Plotner,
https://thehubpwoc.net/2014/09/04/new-bible-studies/

TABLE OF CONTENTS

Part 2: In Christ we are free to...

INTRODUCTION

by Kori Yates

It is for freedom that Christ has set us free. Stand firm, then, and do not let yourselves be burdened again by a yoke of slavery.
Galatians 5:1 NIV

Freedom.

This word in our military culture evokes images of flags, homecomings, ships, helicopters, tanks, and even headstones glistening in the sun. In the military community, we talk of freedom a lot. As a group, we proudly serve our nation and preserve its freedom.

Freedom is a precious commodity we cherish because we understand the cost. With words like liberation, unrestricted, and rights, we've seen and heard real-life stories of those who lack freedom. Freedom is worth the cost both for ourselves and for those who will come behind us. But truly, in all of these ideas, freedom means we've been freed FROM something.

There is no freedom without slavery. Whether offered to people or exhorted by ideals, there is no need for freedom if there has never been slavery. It is the stark contrast to restriction and fear that makes freedom a cherished commodity.

As Christ-followers, freedom is a part of life and of salvation. The Bible states that Christ has set us free, but it's vital that we understand the scope of our freedom. He has set us free from separation; the great divide between a righteous God and a sinful man was bridged by Christ alone. With Christ as Lord, separation from God is no more.

1

Think of what threatens to entangle you – jealousy, fear, sadness, anger, addictions, confusion, and so much more.

We *have been* set free.

But "freedom" doesn't mean "free for all."

By God's design, freedom comes with boundaries. As much as we sometimes wish to just do what we want, the Lord establishes boundaries with love and care for his most precious creation and for the furtherance of his Kingdom.

Boundaries are good.

In our culture, we struggle with boundaries. As Americans, we love freedom in all its varieties, but wrestle with accepting lines drawn between the freedoms we want personally, and those we want to restrict for others.

Example? Free speech is a wonderful thing until someone's untrue "speech" ruins a career, tears apart a family, or brings down a reputation. Freedom to say whatever we want doesn't seem quite so fair in those instances.

God figured it out long ago. He has set boundaries to our freedom as Christians, not because he enjoys restrictions, but because he loves us. These boundaries give us protection, guidance, and even hope. Freedom is not a burden; it's a privilege. We have freedom from much, but in return we're required to be obedient to the One who set us free.

Galatians 5:1 tells us, "It is for freedom that Christ has set us free. Stand firm, then, and do not let yourselves be burdened again by a yoke of slavery" (NIV). In these pages we remember what we have been set free *from* and what we have been set free *to*. We will be challenged to boldly follow the One who set us free. It is an adventure, for sure, but a worthy one.

We are FREE. We can be BRAVE because of the One who set us free. Be brave with me and together we will impact a world.

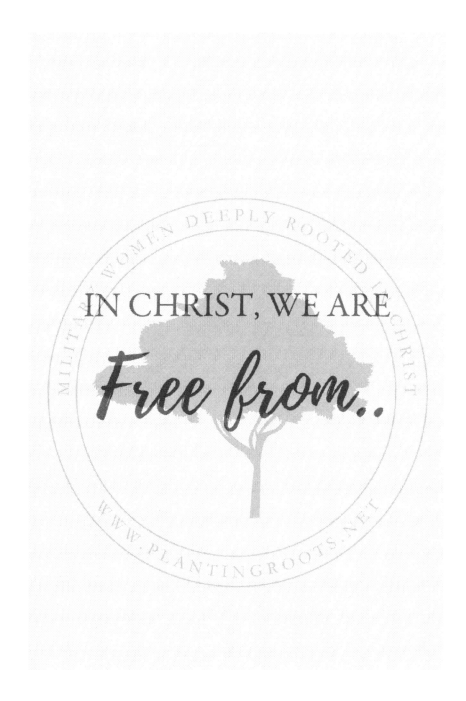

1

FREE FROM BONDAGE

by Kori Yates

There is nothing like the privilege of freedom.

God has set us free from more than we will ever know. He has rescued us from circumstances and feelings easily entangle us, but he has also rescued us, diverted us, and freed us from things by never letting us encounter them. Our freedom is undeserved and surely something we could never achieve on our own, but it was worth the price to God.

Our freedom came at a cost.

A high cost.

Are you grateful for the freedom Christ has given us? We are thankful for mercy, grace, hope, and so many other blessing that free us from the bondage of sin. It is truly a gift and one we could never repay; yet this gift comes with responsibility.

The words "stand firm" give us a picture of what that responsibility might look like:

It is for freedom that Christ has set us free. Stand firm, then, and do not let yourselves be burdened again by a yoke of slavery (Galatians 5:1 NIV).

Growing up in north Texas, tornadoes were a part of life. I remember many times over the years spending hours in the hallway at school or in the bathtub at our house with my brother's mattress covering our bodies. Crazy times.

When I was six years old, we had the biggest tornado I have ever experienced. At 6pm on a Tuesday evening in April, my siblings and I were hanging out in the bathtub. My dad came home from work, knowing the storm was coming. Rushing in the front door, he told us to get in the car. We never got in the car in storms like this, but this time we did.

Heading out of the house, I remember my dad holding my hand, the wind pushing so strong that my feet wouldn't stay on the ground.

We climbed in the car and drove a few blocks away. Sitting in the parking lot of a nearby church, we watched three tornadoes become one and roll through our town like nothing I'd ever seen. As we drove home to check on our house, I remember the eerie, unreal feeling of counting streets because there were no landmarks or streets signs to tell us where we were. Fortunately, our house was fine with only a few shingles missing and a tree down. I'll will never forget that storm that showed me the strength and love of my dad.

Reading Galatians 5:1 where Paul tells us to "stand firm," I realize that there is a responsibility that comes with my freedom in Christ. I think back to that day in our front yard when my dad was holding my hand. The wind did not blow me away even though it was fierce. I was safe and sound, not because I was big and strong, but because I held on to my father who was. He held me, keeping me safe in the face of danger.

Standing firm, being BRAVE, is just that. It's holding on to the One who is stronger and letting him hold on to us. We don't have the strength or size to weather the storms on our own. Being BRAVE is a responsibility that comes with our freedom.

How to Stand Firm:

1. **Obey God.** Our freedom in Christ means we remain obedient. We do what he has called us to do and we do it with our whole heart, wherever God has placed us.

2. **Hold on to Christ.** A hand reaches out to us, his Spirit walks with us. Storms and victories are part of life. We simply need to hold on to God who remains consistent and stable in every circumstance.

3. **Be BRAVE.** Freedom means we are free to hope, love, trust, persevere, share Christ... free to do *so many* things. We are FREE to be BRAVE, to boldly step into places beyond our abilities because it's where he has called us.

Storms will come for all of us. The Christian life isn't easy, but it's vital to remember that we are simply responsible for our own obedience—not the results, the responses, or the reactions. We have been given much, but with it comes a responsibility to live out what we believe in a world that needs to know Christ. The strength, faithfulness, and love of our Savior makes us FREE to be BRAVE.

Together, let's take a look at how freedom in Christ plays out in real time—including the challenges we face in military life. Sisters, let's band together, encouraging one another to stand firm Christ and reminding each other to choose BRAVE. Where will he take us? What will he ask of us? Only the Lord knows. If we boldly live what we believe, holding on to faith, we will leave a legacy of Christ. Our fearless faith will show others the power of freedom in Christ. What could be better?

Our heart is to be FREE TO BE BRAVE.

From what has Christ set you free? Do the boundaries of your freedom frustrate or inspire you? What is he asking you to do today?

Verses to Consider

For you were called to freedom, brethren; only do not turn your freedom into an opportunity for the flesh, but through love serve one another. (Galatians 5:13 NASB)

Live as people who are free, not using your freedom as a cover-up for evil, but living as servants of God. (1 Peter 2:16)

See to it that no one takes you captive by philosophy and empty deceit, according to human tradition, according to the elemental spirits of the world, and not according to Christ. (Colossians 2:8)

Prayer

Lord, help me to stand firm regardless of the circumstances around me. I'm grateful for the freedom I have in you. Help me bravely follow wherever you lead. Amen.

2

FREE FROM WEARINESS

by Muriel Gregory

Adversity is a fact of life.

Truly, truly, I say to you, unless a grain of wheat falls into the earth and dies, it remains alone; but if it dies, it bears much fruit. (John 12:24)

Crushed dreams, shattered expectations, broken hearts, ruptured trust. Life is hard. As I am aging, the lines on my face are reminders of some tough times. The lines between my eyebrows have been carved in by deployment worries, the anguish of a teenager driving on their own for the first time, and those times when we had more bills than paycheck.

Other times have carved different lines. Stretch marks are my badge of honor for having children, a true blessing in my life. The laughing lines around my eyes are the testimony of good times celebrated with friends and family. As I continue to age, those lines will continue to be carved in, a constant reminder of good times and bad times.

On our worst days, life can seem unbearable. We become weary of the moves, the constant loss of friendships, the never-ending deployment cycle. We are drained from being a single parent with no relative close by to lend a hand. We are jaded from hauling enough curtains to fit any type of windows.

We are worn from smiling at every change of command and award ceremony because our heart is screaming, "I have had enough!"

Hardship brings weariness that can cause us to look down and quit or look up and cry out, "How long, Father, how long?"

There is an unspeakable beauty and joy that comes from bringing our crushed dreams, shattered expectations and broken hearts to God.

- He welcomes our weariness and replaces it with his personal light load (Matthew 11:28).

- He reminds us that the work he started in us will be completed (Philippians 1:6).

- He admonishes us of our weakness because our strength comes from him (2 Corinthians 12:10).

- He invites us to come and follow him (Luke 9:23).

- He bids us to die with him.

Our God radically wants the best for you. Your choice is radical as well: surrender to him every day. "Truly, truly, I say to you, unless a grain of wheat falls into the earth and dies, it remains alone; but if it dies, it bears much fruit" (John 12:24).

Dying to self is the cure for everything. It will cure:

- Your weariness

- Your sense of loss

- Your feeling of worthlessness

- Your identity crisis

Dying to self replaces the weariness with *Christ in you, the hope of glory.* (Colossians 1:27)

When you allow your tarnished dreams and your broken heart to die in the hands of a loving Savior, good things will happen. I know too well the temptation to give up, quit, leave everything.

I'm familiar with the deep feeling of weariness that eats up your soul and wrecks your body.

The lines on my face are my reminders.

However, God has been more intimate with me during those times than any other. When I hit rock bottom, Jesus became my bottom line and my saving grace. Mountaintops are for the view but fruits are grown in the valley.

When I die to self, I am free to be brave in a broken world.

How to Be Free from Weariness:

1. **Seek his kingdom** first (Matthew 6:33).

2. **Pick up your cross** (your burden, your weariness) and follow Christ (learn from him, follow his ways, obey his commands). (Luke 9:23).

3. **Trust in his promise** of rest (Matthew 11:28). In order to follow God, we must come to him. When we come to God, he promises us rest.

4. **Look for joy.** The laugh of a baby. The song of a bird. A beautiful sunrise. Coffee shared with a friend. Actively be on the lookout for these instances of God's blessing.

When you feel weary, call out to your Heavenly Father. Ask him to bring to mind a friend to call. Look around for the blessings that remind you of your Father and his gifts to you.

Verses to Consider

"Come to me, all you who are weary and burdened, and I will give you rest." (Matthew 11:28 NIV)

"But we have this treasure in jars of clay to show that this all-surpassing power is from God and not from us. We are hard pressed on every side, but not crushed; perplexed, but not in despair; persecuted, but abandoned; struck down, but not destroyed." (2 Corinthians 4:7-9)

"I rejoiced greatly in the Lord.... for I have learned to be content whatever the circumstances. I know what it is to be in need, and I know what it is to have plenty. I have learned the secret of being content in any and every situation, whether well fed or hungrey, whether living in plenty or in want. I can do all this through him who gives me strength." (Philippians 4:11-13)

Prayer

Lord, I pray that I will be brave enough to bring my brokenness, fully trusting that you will turn it into something beautiful. Thank you for being my strength, when I am weak and my song when I can't speak. Amen.

3

FREE FROM FAILURE

by Kristen Goodrich

Each of us who has worn a uniform or who is currently serving had to go through boot camp. My first-hand transition from civilian to military life happened one hot, humid summer in Maryland. Just showing up for my swearing in required a measure of bravery.

My six-week boot camp experience offered frequent opportunities fail. Being brave required me to draw on strength beyond myself. My will, my pride, my competitive spirit could only take me so far as I faced hurdles beyond my ability.

Quickly, I learned to look for additional strength – and I found such strength in my always-present Savior, Jesus Christ. Through him, I was able to do things I found too daunting.

I can do all things through him who strengthens me.
(Philippians 4:13)

- Choices I had taken for granted were now dictated by my squad leader – what to wear, when to eat, and even how to speak

- Challenges that seemed too hard were now mandatory— jumping off the ten-meter dive platform, calling cadence, learning basic seamanship and navigation...

- And compatriots whom I would have avoided became my roommates, my squadmates, and my shipmates.

During boot camp, being brave meant putting my blistered feet into dorky athletic socks, taking a deep breath, and then shoving those sore feet into newly-acquired footgear designed by the lowest bidder on a government contract.

Since then, I have repeatedly pushed through physical pain. I've swum a mile wearing my khaki uniform shirt and trousers. I've been on the remedial PT squad for failing my push-ups – more than once. I've twice missed maxing my run time by only two seconds.

Each of these moments of perseverance added another layer to my foundation of brave, increasing my confidence.

In boot camp, being brave meant gathering my wits and finding the courage to step out into passageways filled with screaming squad leaders. We weren't allowed to leave our rooms unless all those in the room left together, so we had to collectively take a deep breath and head into the "scary" together.

Every day of boot camp included group challenges and opportunities to let one another down:

- Missing a tasker such as changing uniforms.

- Wrestling with a possible honor violation.

- Being ranked last or facing a possible review board.

Even when I missed the mark, my fellow newbies stood with me, at times holding me up mentally. Banding together, we can be brave when we have others standing alongside.

At night during boot camp, falling asleep was either instantaneous oblivion or next to impossible. Restless nights hung heavy with worry about the past day's failures or fear of the next day's pain. I began to read a couple of sentences in a devotional book I was allowed to bring. Agitation gave way to peace as I read a Bible verse or a sentence describing a basic spiritual truth.

Through the days (and nights) of boot camp, I said many *help-me-now prayers*, enjoyed the air-conditioning at chapel, and fell into the practice of walking with Jesus. He has been ever-faithful throughout my journey from recruit to graduate, from specialty course to initial assignments, from being issued my DD-214 separation from military service to being issued my retiree dependent ID card.

How to Be Free From Failure

Rely on the strength of Christ when you need to be brave. The lessons in courage I learned in boot camp have held true beyond uniformed military life. These are ways that Christ has faithfully strengthened me again and again. The power of Christ frees me from fear of failure.

1. **Speak aloud the truth of Scripture.** Find your brave and use your voice to claim this promise from Philippians 4:13: *I can do all things through him who strengthens me.*

2. **Stand together**. Don't leave your friends when the going gets tough—help others rely on the strength of Christ as well. We are stronger together.

3. **Keep in step with the Spirit** (Galatians 5:25). Walk through every day and every night with our faithful companion, Jesus Christ.

Even though I haven't worn a uniform in decades, I continue practice bravery by pushing myself physically by taking on new challenges. Most recently, I signed up for beginner classical ballet classes, a new kind of physical training. Not to mention that pink tights are also out of my comfort level!

Staying in the hospital room as loved ones take their last breath on earth isn't easy. But bravery pays dividends as I treasure the blessing of sitting with others in the midst of deep, emotional pain.

Walking with Jesus means I've had fewer restlessness nights as well as more peaceful days. Notice I didn't say life got easier.

---

*But life is **richer** with Jesus.*

Acknowledge how fear of failure may be impacting you. Find a way to challenge yourself this week in the physical, emotional, and/or spiritual arenas. Experience for yourself the blessings of being brave!

Verses to Consider

Your word is a lamp to my feet and a light to my path. (Psalm 119:105)

Do you not know that in a race all the runners run, but only one receives the prize? So run that you may obtain it. (1 Corinthians 9:24)

Wait for the LORD; be strong, and let your heart take courage; wait for the LORD! (Psalm 27:14)

Prayer

Lord, thank you for challenging me to be brave! When I find my strength in you, I am free from fear of failure. With you walking by my side, I know that I can push through pain, stand when the going gets tough, and trust you to keep me on the path you've set before me, whether in uniform or not. Amen.

The Midshipman's Prayer –

Almighty Father,

Whose way is in the Sea,

Whose Paths are in the Great Waters,

Whose Command is over all and

Whose Love never faileth;

Let me be aware of Thy Presence and

Obedient to Thy Will.

Keep me True to my best self,

Guarding me against dishonesty in Purpose and in Deed,

And helping me so to live that

I can stand unashamed and unafraid before

My Shipmates, My Loved Ones, and Thee.

Protect those in whose Love I Live.

Give me the Will to do my best and to accept my share of

Responsibilities with a Strong Heart and a Cheerful Mind.

Make me considerate of those Entrusted to my Leadership and

Faithful to the Duties my Country has Entrusted to me.

Let my Uniform remind me daily of the

Traditions of the service of which I am a part.

If I am inclined to doubt, steady my faith;

If I am tempted, make me strong to resist;

If I miss the mark, give me courage to try again.

Guide me with the Light of Truth

And keep before me the

Life of Him by Whose example and help I trust to obtain the

Answer to my Prayer,

Jesus Christ our Lord.

Amen.

4

FREE FROM THE PAST

by Ginger Harrington

A few years ago, several women met to talk about big dreams, casting a vision for the future. With our eyes on God, we prayed and planned, reaching toward a calling far too big for any one of us to accomplish on our own.

As we began to move forward, it took faith to imagine the dream was possible. This was the January day that Planting Roots became more than an idea. This was the beginning of a God-sized adventure.

For me personally, this opportunity came during a season of discouragement. Fear and anxiety had been frequent visitors robbing me of peace in too many military transitions. Tempted to hold back, I realized I didn't want to play it safe, continuing to carry the regrets of the past. As a new calling inspired a new direction, these words from Philippians 3 spoke life and courage to my soul:

No, dear brothers and sisters, I have not achieved it, but I focus on this one thing: Forgetting the past and looking forward to what lies ahead, I press on to reach the end of the race and receive the heavenly prize for which God, through Christ Jesus, is calling us. (Philippians 3:13-14 NLT)

Single-minded focus begins with our thoughts, but also includes our priorities. I'm discovering that there's both a mental and spiritual discipline to letting go of the past. Today defines the distance between yesterday and tomorrow, and it is faith that fills the gap.

Many of our past things are good, blessings like a great duty station, a welcoming neighborhood, a successful work environment, a promotion, good health, or happy kids. Feelings of shame, discouragement, or guilt based on past history do not have to weigh us down, making it hard to move forward.

We need to remember that mistakes made in the past do not have to dictate the future. Focusing on the past is walking backwards into tomorrow.

Here's what I'm learning: courage and freedom are not found in the past. They are sacred gifts for the present, received when we keep our focus and priority on trusting God. Between past and future, we have this decision in our hands today—the choice to trust God and rely on his provision as we make our next steps, decisions, and plans.

How will today look different if you focus on the priority of God's call for your life? He offers a divine invitation to be free from the thoughts, beliefs, habits, and actions that entrap us in the past rather. Making us brave, God empowers us to stretch forward with faith and courage.

God's upward call includes his desire for each of us to be free from the past by relying on Christ to lead us forward. Let's make the choice to be intentional with our thoughts, goals, and desires.

By faith, receive courage to do what is right and face forward as you press on to that one thing that makes all the difference. Relying on Christ is one holy choice for every moment.

Let this truth fortify your heart with courage to let go of the past and embrace the future.

Because we're forgiven. . .

Because we're loved. . .

Because we're free. . .

We can be brave, knowing we have the power of God leading us.

How to Be Free from the Past:

Evaluate your focus—where are you directing your attention?

1. **Look forward**. Don't allow the past consume your focus today.

2. **See your future** in light of the promises of God.

3. **Press on** by relying on Christ each day.

4. **Do the next thing** God asks of you.

Prayerfully consider if you are holding on to something from your past that keeps you from moving forward in faith. What is one thing you can do today to trust God with your future?

Verses to Consider

Therefore, since we have so great a cloud of witnesses surrounding us, let us also lay aside every encumbrance and the sin which so easily entangles us, and let us run with endurance the race that is set before us, fixing our eyes on Jesus, the author and perfecter of faith, who for the joy set before Him endured the cross, despising the shame, and has sat down at the right hand of the throne of God. (Hebrews 12:1-2 NASB)

But seek first His kingdom and His righteousness, and all these things will be added to you. (Matthew 6:33 NASB)

Delight yourself in the LORD, and he will give you the desires of your heart. Commit your way to the LORD: trust in him, and he will act. (Psalm 37:4-5)

Prayer

Lord, show me any area of life where I'm looking to the past in a way that hinders my growth in Christ. Today, I choose to focus forward with my attention and faith centered on you. Amen.

5

FREE FROM I SHOULD

by Brenda Pace

On too many days than I care to count, my self-talk begins, "You really should be farther along in your spiritual walk." Or, "This is not something that should upset you!" Or, "You should be able respond to this challenge without so many doubts about yourself."

Do you see the common denominator in all my *shoulds*?

Me.

I'm the common denominator. Each struggle begins and ends with me: my response and subsequent effort with the focus on failure.

We can move from failure to freedom.

The apostle Paul writes in 2 Corinthians 3:17, "Now the Lord is the Spirit, and where the Spirit of the Lord is, **there is freedom**" (NIV emphasis added).

This freedom is not a license to be released from accountability. Paul writes of freedom that transforms my introspection into a reflection of the glory of Christ.

But we all, with unveiled face beholding as in a mirror the glory of the Lord, are being transformed into the same image from glory to glory, just as from the Lord, the Spirit. (2 Corinthians 3:18 NASB)

Did you catch the detail that transformation is an ongoing process? I can get stuck on not meeting my goals. Praise God, Scripture declares transformation as a process of one degree of glory to another. That tells me I *should* not be surprised when doubts arise. *Yes, there are some sanctified "shoulds!"*

When the process feels like I've only moved forward one-tenth of one degree, it helps to ask myself where I would be without God working in my heart.

True freedom is living and walking in the Spirit. This happens for me as I read and study God's Word, trusting him to direct my thoughts, strengthen my emotions, and help me do the right thing.

Too often I view the Spirit as being with me and every now and then I turn around to give him a high-five. Walking in the Spirit isn't merely a casual greeting—it is allowing the Spirit to guide me step by step. No, I don't want a Holy Spirit high-five; I want a Holy Spirit embrace!

How to Be Free from "I Should":

1. **Acknowledge limitations** and recognize where you would be without the Holy Spirit's work in your life.

2. **Trust the Spirit** through prayer as you begin each day, asking him to guide you.

3. **Recognize the Spirit** is not just beside you, but he lives within you.

4. **Give credit to the Spirit of God** for any good in you.

In her book *Free of Me,* author Sharon Hodde Miller refers to Moses and Jeremiah, who both battled self-confidence and personal weakness. Read their stories and you can imagine Moses saying, "I *should* talk better," or Jeremiah saying, "I *should* be more mature."

Miller writes that God did not respond to these men and their struggles with self-help talks as we do so often with one another today. She points out that God did not affirm their leadership, talents, or gifts. He didn't give them a hug, praise their efforts, or speak encouraging words over them. She concludes, "God didn't do any of those things, but instead he changed the subject. God affirmed his own strength, his own leadership, his own self.[1]"

Why? Because the outcome did not rest upon human ability but upon the greatness of God. The transforming Spirit of God frees us from the "I should" syndrome that depends on our abilities as He releases us to rely on God's power.

What are some of the "I shoulds" that can hold you captive?

How has God used military life in the process of your spiritual transformation?

Verses to Consider

There is therefore now no condemnation for those who are in Christ Jesus. (Romans 8:1)

Who shall bring any charge against God's elect? It is God who justifies. Who is to condemn? Christ Jesus is the one who died— more than that, who was raised—who is at the right hand of God, who indeed is interceding for us. (Romans 8:33-34)

Prayer

Lord, show me what is holding me captive. Free me from worrying about "I shoulds" and doubts. Remind me of your Spirit and how he is guiding me and walking beside me. Amen.

See appendix for additional resources on this topic.

---

[1] Sharon Hodde Miller, Free of Me, Baker Books: Grand Rapids, 2017, p. 46.

6

FREE FROM THE PERFORMANCE PRISON

by Ginger Harrington

What do you do when performance becomes a prison?

My good friend stands at the mailbox, holding the weight of too many burdens on her shoulders. I can tell she's had a difficult day as I stop to say hello. Knowing my neighbors is one of the things I like about base housing. I ask her how things are going.

"I try so hard to be a good mom, but I feel like I'm not doing it right," she says with a shrug. "It's a constant challenge to give my best at work in a busy command. The kids bicker and fight all the time. I'm working harder than I've ever worked, but it feels like there's nothing to show for it."

With a weary sigh, she says, "Sorry, I didn't mean to dump on you. I just need to work harder to get it all together. I'm trying to be a better mom, soldier, and Christian, but . . ." Without words, her body language finishes the sentence that hangs in the air: *but I'm not.*

How well I know this struggle as I listen to the discouragement in my friend's weary words. Do you know it too?

We get hung up on doing things right—performing well in our responsibilities and roles. There's an additional stress for women in uniform due to military culture—surpassing standards, following rules, and excelling on the job are very real pressures in unit morale and command structure.

God wants us to know that our identity in Christ sets us free from the pressure of trying to earn his favor and get ourselves together through our own efforts. Spiritually, the performance prison is a trap of self-righteousness, a way of living where we are constantly trying to get it all together and do it all right.

Have you noticed the struggle inherent in this way of living? It is a subtle form of self-righteousness, and the trouble is we never know if we've made it. How much is enough?

Performance-based faith leaves us insecure, for we're never free and rarely at rest. Freedom is found when self-effort gives way to faith.

Out of sheer generosity he put us in right standing with himself. A pure gift. He got us out of the mess we're in and restored us to where he always wanted us to be. And he did it by means of Jesus Christ. (Romans 3:24 MSG)

God clarified my understanding of **righteousness** when I read this definition: "the state of him who is *as he ought to be,* righteousness, the condition acceptable to God." It includes integrity, virtue, purity of life, rightness, correctness *of thinking, feeling, and acting* (Strong's 1343).

He saved us, not on the basis of deeds which we have done in righteousness, but according to His mercy, by the washing of regeneration and renewing by the Holy Spirit. (Titus 3:5 NASB)

When it all depends on our ability to be good enough, the toil of corralling our wayward soul is exhausting. Relentless self-effort quickly entraps us in bondage to performance and perfectionism.

"This is the struggle of self-righteousness—trying to make ourselves right apart from God. This is the war our flesh wages against our spirit, leaving us weary and wounded on battlefields of independence and self-effort. Too often, we twist holiness into self-imposed molds of perfectionism dressed up for Sunday and lurking behind our efforts to please God."[2]

---

[2] Ginger Harrington , *Holy in the Moment: Simple Ways to Love God and Enjoy Your Life* (Nashville: Abingdon Press, 2018) 70.

How to Be Free from the Performance Prison:

1. **Embrace the truth** that you *are* holy and righteous. When you worry about working harder to get it all together, remember righteousness is a gift of identity and not a reward for good performance.

2. **Rely on Christ in your efforts.** Invite Christ into your work and relationships, "Lord, help me in all my work. Express your righteousness in all I do today."

3. **Surrender your roles to God.** Trust him with the people and responsibilities in your life.

4. **Rest the outcomes of your efforts in God's capable hands** and let go the stress of performance. Work hard, but resist the temptation to worry about the results.

5. **Recognize when you are trying to control circumstances** by trying harder in your own effort.

It's easy to mentally assent to the truth that righteousness is our identity in Christ. But when self-effort kicks in, we discover there is a subtle shift to self-righteousness and performance. I struggle with this more than I'd like, but God helps me make practical choices to find freedom from the work of trying to do everything right.

Try these intentional choices to find freedom from performance and self-righteousness.

What would it look like for you to step out of the trap of performing for acceptance and approval from God or from others?

Verses to Consider

Be renewed in the spirit of your mind, and put on the new self, which in the likeness of God has been created in righteousness and holiness of the truth. (Ephesians 4:23-24 NASB)

He made Him who knew no sin to be sin on our behalf, so that we might become the righteousness of God in Him. (2 Corinthians 5:21 NASB)

For if by the transgression of the one, death reigned through the one, much more those who receive the abundance of grace and of the gift of righteousness will reign in life through the One, Jesus Christ. (Romans 5:17 NASB)

Prayer

Lord, thank you for the gift of righteousness that sets me free from the prison of self-effort and performance-based faith. I choose to rely on you to work in every area of my life. Remind me to choose freedom when I feel the pressure to perform for your favor or the approval of people. Amen.

See appendix for additional resources on this topic.

7

FREE FROM THE FEAR OF AGING

by Brenda Pace

On the recent occasion of turning older (*ahem, cough-cough*), I revisited goals I set several years ago when I could no longer deny the mantle of "seasoned woman" was mine to wear.

Because of the younger demographic of military communities in which I move, this *all of a sudden, I'm a Titus II woman* happened much earlier than I expected.

I remember commenting to a friend that I had been described as a "seasoned woman" more times than I care to count. She replied that it meant I'm "spicy" and assured me that was a good thing. (Along with growing older, I'm also working on trusting comments made by friends.)

I'm relieved that God's Word has much to say about growing old. I've struggled with the fear that age means irrelevancy and uselessness, a common implication in today's culture.

However, Psalm 92 declares the following:

The righteous will flourish like a palm tree, they will grow like a cedar of Lebanon; planted in the house of the LORD, they will flourish in the courts of our God. They will still bear fruit in old age, they will stay fresh and green, proclaiming, "The Lord is upright; he is my Rock, and there is no wickedness in him." (Psalm 92:12-15 NIV)

The scriptural principle in Psalm 92 is that I am to celebrate the process of growing older. *Say what?*

Yes, I can *even* increase in usefulness to God's Kingdom and grow stronger because of my deep spiritual roots! Did you know that age makes other things decay, but it makes a palm tree flourish? In fact, the best fruit comes from an older tree.

To those of you still in the prime of youth, it may be tempting to think this message doesn't apply to you. May I remind you of this truth: you are who you are becoming.

The choices you make today will make a difference in how you embrace the process of growing older. Life is an aging process and it's never too early to look to the future.

How to Be Free from the Fear of Aging:

Here are some things that have helped me embrace the inevitability of age.

1. **Study scripture** on the topic of age. The Bible has much to say about growing old—and discounting Ecclesiastes 12:3, *Your body will grow feeble, your teeth will decay, and your eyesight fail...* it's mostly positive! Consider the lives of women like Sarah, Naomi, Elizabeth, and Anna. These women served God with enthusiasm and purpose even as they advanced in years. What kind of "old" women do you want to become?

2. **Establish and revisit goals.** I think in terms of the future and ask myself what do I want to be or do in five, ten, or twenty years? What will I regret if I don't pursue? What will keep me healthy in spirit, mind, and body as the years progress?

3. **Invest in eternity.** The things that are eternal include people and God's Word. Relationships are more important to me now than ever before. I pray for opportunities to share the truth of God's Word through my words and actions. I want to be known as a woman who loved God and others well.

4. **Remember that spiritual gifts do not cease**. The words of Billy Graham ring true, "There is no retirement mentioned in the Bible."[3] In a spiritual sense a woman's (true) work is never done.

5. **Challenge yourself** to keep moving forward. Scripture promises we can go from strength to strength (Psalm 84:7) and glory to glory (2 Corinthians 3:18). I choose to be a lifelong learner, challenging myself to keep growing in areas of life and godliness.

Verses to Consider

Even to your old age and gray hairs I am he, I am he who will sustain you. I have made you and I will carry you; I will sustain you and I will rescue you. (Isaiah 46:4 NIV)

Is not wisdom found among the aged? Does not long life bring understanding? (Job 12:12)

Likewise, teach the older women to be reverent in the way they live, not to be slanderers or addicted to much wine, but to teach what is good. Then they can urge the younger women to love their husbands and children, to be self-controlled and pure, to be busy at home, to be kind, and to be subject to their husbands, so that no one will malign the Word of God. (Titus 2:3-5)

---

[3] John Charles Pollack, *The Billy Graham Story: The Authorized Biography* (Grand Rapids: Zondervan, 1985), 310.

Prayer

Lord, release me from fear of growing older. Help me look to the future with courage, knowing that even to my old age you will be the same. And even in my graying years you will bear me (Isaiah 46:4). Use me to bless others and enable me to come to the grave in full vigor of life (Job 5:26). Amen

See appendix for additional resources on this topic.

8

FREE FROM NEED

by Claudia Duff

The losses keep me up at night.

Where did I put that? I lose things a lot, like every day. I say, "I can't find my hairbrush. Where are my keys? Where did I put the __?" Then there are the needs I face and the things I want. In big ways and small, God teaches me to trust him with my needs.

When my husband and I went away to celebrate our 25th wedding anniversary, our kids were old enough to stay home alone for eight days. Don't worry, we didn't break any laws; they were 22, 20 and 18. I stocked the fridge, pantry, and freezer, then ensured the POV had a full tank of gas. We were good to go. I reminded them that there was "emergency money" tucked safely inside the green purse in my closet—only to be used if there was an actual emergency.

A few days into our cruise I got an urgent message from the kids asking, "Mom, which green purse? You have several!" I was able to guide them to the correct purse. Apparently they looked for a couple of days and had even begun calling my friends, asking if they knew which green purse. Once home, I asked, "What was the emergency?"

They answered, "We ran out of food!"

Just for the record, I bought more than enough food to last eight days. But, the boy children stayed up late at night playing video games and managed to eat their way through the food in a matter of three days. Needless to say, my children found themselves in a place need.

Haven't we all been in the same place with regard to our personal walk with God? I know I have. I frequently experience needs of many kinds.

The Lord is teaching me to see what has already been provided.

So David inquired of the LORD, saying, "Shall I pursue this troop? Shall I overtake them?" And He answered him, "Pursue, for you shall surely overtake them and without fail recover all." (1 Samuel 30:8 NKJV)

David struggled with a great loss. To make the situation worse, his defeat came from a fierce enemy. Sitting alone on a pile of ruins that used to be his home, David called out to God.

I love this part of the story:

Now David was greatly distressed, for the people spoke of stoning him, because the soul of all the people was grieved, every man for his sons and his daughters. But David strengthened himself in the LORD his God. (1 Samuel 30:6 NKJV)

The strongest weapon for overcoming an overwhelming situation is to seek the Lord. Sounds simple, but it's not always our first thought—at least it's not usually my first thought.

But David got it. He sought strength in God, encouraging himself in the steadfast character of the Lord. The Lord is teaching me to become brave enough to do the same and to look at my need and seek the Lord for his provision.

I am learning to own my hard places and be honest by saying, "Lord, this is a hard place, what's next?" With bravery, I'm laying my hard places of broken relationships or sinful behavior into the Father's hand.

Most importantly, I'm discovering the power of believing the truth and authority of God's Word. I'm armored up for the battle to believe.

We will be bombarded daily with tough stuff: "These things I have spoken to you, that in me you may have peace. In the world you will have tribulation; but be of good cheer, I have overcome the world" (John 16:33 NKJV).

This is no empty promise! The Word declares victory before we even get started. Sometimes the place of lack, want and need is where we will see the greatest miracles in our lives. Even in our poverty we can gain an eternity of wealth through the sacrifice of ourselves. Our need doesn't determine the size of our gifts as unto the Lord.

How to Be Free from Need:

1. **Own your hard places** by naming them.

2. **Surrender your challenges** to the Lord with an action to lay them in his hands. (*Lord, I give you my anxiety of this broken relationship by asking for their forgiveness. Fill me with your grace.*)

3. **Write a prayer** of thanksgiving, repentance, or declaration of victory--however the Holy Spirit leads.

But wait there's more.

Jesus can only redeem what we place in his hands.

Picture this: your Lord with hands outstretched, reaching for your hard places. Accept his offer, place your needs in the more-than-capable hands of Jesus.

Now walk away.

Verses to Consider

He called to her and said, "Bring me a morsel of bread in your hand." And she said, "As the Lord tour God lives, I have nothing baked, only a handful if flour in a jar and a little oil in a jug."
(1 Kings 17:11-12)

Many rich people out in large sums. And a poor widow came and put in two small copper coins, which make a penny.
(Mark 12:41-44)

Prayer

Lord, I am grateful for my seasons of lack, want, and need. They remind me that I have a Savior who loves to rescue me again and again. Thank you for providing for my needs. Help me to strengthen myself in you. Amen.

9

FREE FROM EXCESS

by Jennifer Wake

Hi ho, hi ho, off to purge I go!

MOVING TIME! That statement always strikes deep into my heart.

Beyond worrying about the new place and finding friends, I start fixating on things. What you should know about me is I come from a family of collectors. For example, my aunt had 2000+ Dachshund models when she passed away.

I seem to start a new collection without even realizing. In fact, I have a spoon collection, a snack tray collection, and an eclectic collection of craft supplies.

I also collect books.

Two moves ago, we had to move everything ourselves since we were "just" moving off post. The distance was short but it was very eye-opening for me. I realized that I had way too much stuff. Especially books, which are very heavy.

That move helped me begin a journey to free myself from excess. The Holy Spirit began to show me about gluttony and overindulgence. The writer of Romans reminds us about what we should be focused on.

But put on the Lord Jesus Christ, and make no provision for the flesh, to gratify its desires. (Romans 13:14)

My gluttony is related to books. I especially love books about God. I realized that I have a tendency to over-focus on what other people write about God rather than spending time myself with God in his Word. For me, I needed to lighten the number of books I was storing.

"To put on the Lord Jesus Christ," means to focus on what he wants you to become. I am learning moderation in things which can distract me from Jesus, even good things like Christian books.

Recently, I spent a weekend pulling books from my "library" shelves. I lined them up in my hallway. I left them there *in case*. You know, *in case* I need a book. *In case* I need to have ideas for ministry or writing. *In case* my husband needs one for a sermon.

I'm still holding on to them, *just in case*. But God is showing me he can provide all things that I need.

How to Free Yourself from Excess:

1. **Prayerfully consider** what you focus on instead of Christ.

2. **Spend time purging** your areas of excess.

3. **Make decisions about what to keep.** I use the three-pile method: trash, donate, and keep.

Pile 1 is labeled "TRASH." These are completed Bible study books or books that are torn. (I used to keep completed study books but I found my journals have more insight.)

Pile 2 is labeled "DONATE." I have collected Bible study books I wanted to look at but have never completed. I give those books to local chapels.

Pile 3 is labeled "KEEP." This one is the smallest. I keep my journals and a few favorite study books that I can reuse.

Put pile 1 in the trash bin, donate pile 2, then organize pile 3.

I use this system every move for going through closets and collections. Getting rid of extra things we really don't need makes moving easier, but more importantly, it frees me from being a slave to my possessions.

What do you have too much of? Craft supplies? Movies? Exercise equipment? Are you hoarding things that have become a distraction or a weight?

As I culled through my overstock of books, I was able to donate several to my local Bible study and chapel which will allow other ladies to learn about God. I know that I have other areas of excess in my life. As I keep my focus on God, I want to live lightly in the Spirit, free from excess.

Verses to Consider

Their end is destruction, their god is their belly, and they glory in their shame, with minds set on earthly things. (Philippians 3:19)

Put to death therefore what is earthly in you: sexual immorality, impurity, passion, evil desire, and covetousness, which is idolatry. (Colossians 3:5)

And he said to them, "Take care, and be on your guard against all covetousness, for one's life does not consist in the abundance of his possessions." (Luke 12:15)

Prayer

Lord, guide me on things that take my focus from you. Help me to not be excessive and guide me to your wisdom when I desire things over you. Thank you for being with me during every season and transition. Amen.

10

FREE FROM FEAR AND ISOLATION

by Claudia Duff

Sometimes the only way out is through.

I used to say to my kids on a regular basis, "Fear is never a good reason to not do something." If I discovered they were afraid of something, I would insist they try.

Lately, I find myself needing those words myself.

Our family is in a long season of transition. It's been an ongoing event for the past six years when my husband retired from the military. Fear of life after the military has been my constant companion far too long.

Sometimes fear merely sat quietly on a shelf in my heart, but at times it was quite vocal. "What if this plan doesn't work? What will you do if that goes sideways? Watch out; the other shoe will eventually drop!"

Fear is an awful taskmaster, requiring our all. All of our faith, all of our desires, all of our energy--just flat all of all. Yet, in return, fear gives us nothing.

You're familiar with these thoughts, I'm sure. Little by little, I'm learning how to shut the murmuring mouth of fear, rendering it powerless in my life. It's easy for fear to hold us captive. This is why I need to meditate on this truth again and again:

For freedom Christ has set us free; stand firm therefore, and do not submit again to a yoke of slavery. (Galatians 5:1)

Retirement from the military has been a steady journey of adjustment. Fear loves change; it's fuel for the fire that ignites anxiety. We've lived in five different homes in four years. I lost my tribe of friends with every move and found myself dreading change of any kind. I began to isolate myself from others, depending on Netflix, Christian books, and my iPod for fellowship and direction.

Not the best plan folks, trust me on this.

Fear dug in and life kept coming at me. I was finally forced to still the voice of anxiety and replace it with some faith. I wish I could say it was just one *come to Jesus* moment but, actually, it was many.

For God gave us a spirit not of fear but of power and love and self-control. (2 Timothy 1:7)

Our God understands the bondage of fear and has given us a great provision for our weakness—his power!

I'm an introvert, to the point where I could train introverts to become more reserved. So, making friends is not my jam, *at all.* I love people--just in small bites and on my own terms. Not very friendly, right? I found it easier to stay home and not answer my phone.

But, God had a much bigger plan with our last move. We found a church that was ALL about connecting believers. They even did a couple of home visits. My extrovert husband was over the moon. But, you know what happened? We connected with new friends and it took very little effort on my part.

I just had to start saying, "Yes."

I started saying "yes" to just about every invitation of coffee, tea, lunch, dinner, etc. And I found myself again. I rediscovered how much I love Jesus and his women.

Fear was still there, but I beat it back with some serious prayer, counsel, Bible reading, quiet-time sitting, and lots of opportunities to choose righteousness. I recovered my *jam*, the power of love and self-control that only comes from our Savior.

How to Break out of Isolation and Fear:

1. **Read your Bible** every single day; even if it's only a verse, *read it.*

2. **Begin your day with prayer** every single day; even if it's a short prayer, *pray it.*

3. **Talk to someone** outside your home every single day, even if it's the UPS man.

4. **Have a download time** every single day, even if it's just to your pet. Make a concerted effort to connect verbally with someone who cares about you daily.

Social media has become the quick platform that we use to communicate, but we need to go deeper in small ways. Be brave to share your day at the dinner table or talk with a friend on the phone. Tell someone about the good, the bad and the ugly. It's important to practice being vulnerable and sympathetic all at the same time.

Daily connections move us from isolation into relationship.

When PCS season arrives make the effort to connect and communicate with others, whether you are the one moving or staying. The military community can be a great place to hide. But, not anymore! Embrace each new season with grace and grit. In Christ, free yourself from fear and its awful sidekick of isolation. Say "yes" to something this week, you'll be surprised!

Verses to Consider

Your word is a lamp to my feet and a light to my path. (Psalm 119:105)

Call to me and I will answer you, and will tell you great and hidden things that you have not known. (Jeremiah 33:3)

Go and stand in the temple and speak to the people all the words of this Life. (Acts 5:20)

Prayer

Lord, I'm grateful for this day. Thank you for victory over sin, death, and the grave. I'm grateful that you are transforming me into the image of Christ. I give you this day and I will not seize one moment back. Have your will, way, and purpose in my life. Amen.

11

FREE FROM GUILT

by Kori Yates

I feel like a horrible friend. When I had a birthday, my friend remembered. She showed up at my door with thoughtful gifts of things I loved. What a special memory.

Now, ask me if I remembered her birthday.

I remembered the day after her birthday, writing a note on my calendar to run by with a gift. My day got crazy and it was a week later when I remembered again. Thinking of these special days and then thinking of a gift are not really my strong point, so I do things like this a lot.

If you think this was a random occurrence in my world, you are sadly mistaken.

My son is ten years old. I wanted to test his independence, so this week I let him walk to baseball on his own and planned to let him come back to the house when he was done. Not really a bad plan, except this was his last practice and his coach used it to give out certificates and awards for end of the season celebration

As my son walked home clutching his award in his hand, you can imagine that I felt like a stellar mom.

Moments like this happen in life and sometimes our mistakes are much bigger than these. When I disappoint others, guilt washes over me and I question how good a friend or mom I actually am. I also start to wonder what kind of Christ-follower I am if I can't love the ones closest to me well.

Guilt. It's a struggle sometimes, but it's not part of his plan for me to dwell on my sins and shortcomings. "As the Father has loved me, so have I loved you. Abide in my love" (John 15:9).

Sometimes these moments are sin and sometimes they are simply part of being human. God is a God of love and grace, and I'm thankful. His love is far beyond our imagination. He invites us to abide, dwell, live in his love, a place of security, hope, joy, and peace. Guilt is not a part of living in peace with God.

Guilt isn't all bad—it has a purpose to help us recognize our sin and seek repentance.

But more often than not for me, guilt comes because I haven't measured up to what I expect of myself, which lands pretty close to perfection.

Abiding in God's love has become an intentional effort, one that is still a work in progress, but some things have helped along the way.

How to Work Through Guilt and Into Love:

1. **Remember truth.** The best way for me to remember truth is to know the truth. Scripture is where that is found. Whether I find specific verses or just read, the Bible makes a difference.

2. **Cultivate godly friendships.** Godly friends are a must, especially if they look at you and say, "I did that just last week!" Genuine friends are a blessing as I realize that others mess up sometimes too.

3. **Choose honesty.** When I mess up, intentional or not, it's best for me just to say so. Doing so puts us back in the game and makes the relationship right again.

4. **Put love into action.** Love is a verb. It's something I do and something the Lord does for me. I work to love well. And although I miss the mark at times, I know God knows my heart and pray others do as well.

Have you messed up lately? Just say so! We're all in this boat together, simply trying to follow Jesus as best we can. Take some time to reflect on how much the Lord loves you, mess ups and all.

Verses to Consider

But you, O Lord, are a God merciful and gracious, slow to anger and abounding in steadfast love and faithfulness. (Psalm 86:15)

For God so loved the world, that he gave his only Son, that whoever believes in him should not perish but have eternal life. (John 3:16)

For this reason I bow my knees before the Father, from whom every family in heaven and on earth is named, that according to the riches of his glory he may grant you to be strengthened with power through his Spirit in your inner being, so that Christ may dwell in your hearts through faith—that you, being rooted and grounded in love, may have strength to comprehend with all the saints what is the breadth and length and height and depth, and to know the love of Christ that surpasses knowledge, that you may be filled with all the fullness of God. (Ephesians 3:14-19)

Prayer

Lord, you are a God of love. Guilt creeps into my heart so easily. Lord, use it to pull me back to you again and be reminded of your great love for me. Amen.

12

FREE FROM HEART DISEASE

by Muriel Gregory

Heart disease is the leading cause of death in the United States. It's likely that you know someone who has either suffered a heart attack.

News reports, blog posts, articles from specialists in the field will tell you that the key risk factors for heart disease are high blood pressure, high cholesterol, diabetes, being overweight, poor diet, physical inactivity, and alcohol abuse.

With that knowledge in hand, many seek to be healthier by eating better, exercising more, quitting smoking, and limiting our alcohol intake. At the same time, we often neglect a less obvious heart disease: *spiritual heart disease.*

Do we have a healthy heart for God? Are we walking in his statutes? Are we devoted to him? Jeremiah 17:9 reminds us that the heart is deceitful above all things and desperately sick. So how do we cure ourselves from spiritual heart disease?

In biblical terms, the heart is the center of things. Deuteronomy 4:11 talks about the heart of heaven, Jonah 2:3 talks about the heart of the sea, and Matthew 12:40 refers to the heart of the earth.

The heart is the home of the personal life. It is the seat of the will (Mark 3:5), the intellect (Mark 2:6,8), and of feeling (Luke 24:32). It is also the seat of conscience, but unfortunately without Christ, it is naturally wicked (Genesis 8:21).

Just like the hardening of your arteries will cause heart disease, the hardening of your spiritual heart will cause you to sin (Proverbs 28:14).

A hardened heart will manifest itself through pride, conceit, ingratitude, and unconcern about God's Word.

The good news is that if you are a Christian, you already hold the cure to your spiritual heart disease. Through prayer, the Holy Spirit can guide you and reveal any area of concern.

How to Exercise Your Heart and Be Free from Heart Disease:

1. **Follow a healthy diet of daily Bible reading and praying.** The truth will set you free (John 8:32) and the truth is found in his Word.

2. **Practice gratitude.** According to an article published by *Newsweek* in 2015, gratitude will keep you healthy, will improve your sleep, and will increase not only your self-esteem but also your empathy and resilience.[4] Grateful people are more hopeful. There are over fifty-two passages mentioning thanksgiving in the Bible. Look them up!

3. **Exercise your spiritual disciplines more often.** To follow Jesus means to practice the disciplines that he practiced. What are those disciplines? Prayer, worship, serving, fasting, silence, and solitude. One book I would recommend on that topic is *Spiritual Disciplines for the Christian Life* by Donald Whitney.

4. **Be filled with the Holy Spirit (Ephesians 5:18).** Very little is taught on the Holy Spirit and yet it is alive inside of us. The same power that raised Jesus from the

---

[4]https://www.newsweek.com/5-scientifically-proven-benefits-gratitude-398582

dead is alive in us. Let's tap into this power to make our hearts more obedient to God.

God wants us to be spiritually healthy. As the great healer, he can perform a heart transplant. The question is, do you want it? We can be free from heart disease. The choice is ours. Living in the freedom of Christ is a lifelong discipline but the rewards are eternal. "And I will give them one heart, and a new spirit I will put within them. I will remove the heart of stone from their flesh and give them a heart of flesh" (Ezekiel 11:19).

Do you recognize the signs of an unhealthy heart? Are you willing to make a change and transform your heart of stone into a heart of flesh? Make a plan and have a friend hold you accountable.

Verses to Consider

You shall therefore lay up these words of mine in your heart and in your soul, and you shall bind them as a sign on your hand, and they shall be as frontlets between your eyes. (Deuteronomy 11:18)

Create in me a clean heart, O God, and renew a right spirit within me. (Psalm 51:10)

Tremble and do not sin; when you are on your beds, search your hearts and be silent. (Psalm 4:4)

I will give them an undivided heart and put a new spirit in them; I will remove from them their heart of stone and give them a heart of flesh. (Ezekiel 11:19)

Prayer

Lord, thank you for your gift of the Holy Spirit. I pray that my heart will be free from pride and conceit and be wholly devoted to you. Amen.

See appendix for an additional resource on this topic.

13

FREE FROM CONFLICT

by Brenda Pace

Do you long to be free from conflict?

Free from conflict—*who am I kidding?* Military life made me no stranger to conflict. I wish a life free from conflict was attainable. Although I have met a few people I'm convinced thrive on strife, to be free of conflict this side of heaven is an impossible dream.

Maybe what I'm really getting at is my need to be free from conflict aversion. When conflict looks remotely possible my first response is to put my fingers in my ears, shut my eyes tight, click my heels, and pray like I'm Dorothy trying to get back home to Kansas.

I may be a peacemaker at heart, but over the years I've often camouflaged my aversion to conflict in the cloak of peacemaking. Thankfully God has used me to promote peace in spite of myself. However, recently I've taken a good inward look and admitted my fear of conflict—as in any way, shape, or form. My courage flees when discord erupts.

I've admitted to myself that often my fear of conflict has owned me and kept me from growing emotionally and spiritually.

I've asked the Lord to teach me discernment for living and working peacefully with people, to make me unafraid to confront or engage in healthy conflict.

I'm reminded of the conflict that ensued between Paul and Barnabas described in Acts 15:36-41:

Some time later Paul said to Barnabas, "Let us go back and visit the believers in all the towns where we preached the word of the Lord and see how they are doing." Barnabas wanted to take John, also called Mark, with them, but Paul did not think it wise to take him, because he had deserted them in Pamphylia and had not continued with them in the work. They had such a sharp disagreement that they parted company. Barnabas took Mark and sailed for Cyprus, but Paul chose Silas and left, commended by the believers to the grace of the Lord. He went through Syria and Cilicia, strengthening the churches. (NIV)

Selfishness does not appear to be the reason for Paul and Barnabas parting ways. Instead they had a disagreement on their views of how to conduct a missionary journey. In fact, they both continued in an effective ministry, perhaps even reaching more people for Christ as they traveled in different directions.

Further, 2 Timothy 4:11 indicates Paul reconciled with John-Mark and Colossians 4:10 gives evidence that Paul and Barnabas remained friends. That's evidence that conflict does not have to be negative.

How to Be Free from Conflict:

1. **Consider the motive.** Conflict is not necessarily negative. What makes it so is the motive behind the conflict. I'm learning to ask myself if the purpose for a conflict is for my or another's selfish reason such as revenge, self-righteousness, and saving face, or is confrontation necessary for a positive change for higher good.

2. **Consider the method.** An attempt to resolve conflict with another must first be done privately to combat misunderstanding, rumors, and assumptions. The biblical model of approaching conflict is found in

Matthew 18:15-17. Too often we speak to others about a conflict before we confront the source. The goal is always to resolve conflict quickly with the least amount of damage as possible. This is counter to today's culture that thrives on conflict with the goal of defeating those who have an opposing view rather than finding a good solution for all.

3. **Consider the outcome**. I've experienced the joy that comes from resolved conflict and I've experienced the heartache that comes from unresolved conflict. When I consider the outcome, I'm motivated to overcome my aversion to conflict and take purposeful steps toward peace.

The reality is that peace is not always up to me. Yet, I am responsible to address conflict in a manner that is honorable.

Engaging in any great or small conflict is a vulnerable act, but I must be willing to live out the words of Romans 12:18, "If possible, so far as it depends on you, live peaceably with all."

Our military often serves in areas of the world as peacekeepers with the goal of creating conditions that favor lasting peace among nations. The overarching goal of a peacekeeping force is to provide security. How does conflict threaten your security?

What do you think Paul meant when he wrote Romans 12:18? What is one thing you can do in your corner of the world to "live at peace with everyone?"

Verses to Consider

So then let us pursue what makes for peace and for mutual upbuilding. (Romans 14:19)

What causes quarrels and what causes fights among you? Is it not this, that your passions are at war within you? You desire and do not have, so you murder. You covet and cannot obtain, so you fight and quarrel. You do not have, because you do not ask. You ask and do not receive, because you ask wrongly, to spend it on your passions. (James 4:1-3)

If your brother sins against you, go and tell him his fault, between you and him alone. If he listens to you, you have gained your brother. But if he does not listen, take one or two others along with you, that every charge may be established by the evidence of two or three witnesses. If he refuses to listen to them, tell it to the church. And if he refuses to listen even to the church, let him be to you as a Gentile and a tax collector. (Matthew 18:15-17)

Prayer

The military promotes *esprit de corps*, which indicates a common spirit that inspires enthusiasm and devotion. Conflict threatens such unity. May the *Peace Prayer of Saint Francis of Assisi* be a guiding force in your life today.

Lord, make me an instrument of your peace:
where there is hatred, let me sow love;
where there is injury, pardon;
where there is doubt, faith;
where there is despair, hope;
where there is darkness, light;
where there is sadness, joy.

O divine Master, grant that I may not so much seek
to be consoled as to console,
to be understood as to understand,
to be loved as to love.
For it is in giving that we receive,
it is in pardoning that we are pardoned,

and it is in dying that we are born to eternal life. Amen.[5]

See appendix for additional resources on this topic.

---

[5] https://www.crosswalk.com/faith/prayer/prayers/the-prayer-of-st-francis-make-me-an-instrument.html

FREE TO BE BRAVE

14

FREE FROM INNER CHAOS

by Muriel Gregory

Feeling stressed?

We've all faced stressful days that hold our peace of mind hostage. When multiple stressors converge, stress can get the best of us. For me, May 2002 was a busy month. I gave birth to our third child four days after taking my finals for college. June was a blur. I adjusted to being a mom to three young ones. I was taking my last required classes online and packing the house for an upcoming PCS. All this while my husband was away on TDY.

I don't remember much of July 2002. My sanity was more than likely gone. All I know is that I kept the kids alive and that we were PCS ready when my husband came home.

The birth of a child, moving, and finishing school all belong to life's top stressors. It's fair to say that the military offers more stressful opportunities than most other lifestyles.

There are countless studies and articles discussing the effect of stress on military members and military families. From PTSD to suicide, domestic violence to divorce, stress can be extremely destructive.

Since stress is unavoidable, how do we deal with it?

I love the image of Jesus sleeping in the middle of a storm even as the boat is being swamped by the waves: "And behold, there arose a great storm on the sea so that the boat was being swamped by the waves; but he [Jesus] was asleep" (Matthew 8:24, clarification added). What a beautiful picture of equanimity. Defined as evenness of mind, especially under stress, equanimity is finding peace in the midst of what life throws at you. Jesus displayed self-control, composure, and calm in the midst of a

61

dangerous storm. His example reveals a secret to freedom in the grip of fear, Jesus promises to give us his peace: "Peace I leave with you; my peace I give to you. Not as the world gives do I give to you. Let not your hearts be troubled, neither let them be afraid" (John 14:27).

The reality is that we *can* rest and not fret when our boat gets swamped by the storms of life. Peace is not the absence of stressors, issues, or problems, peace is the assurance and gift of Christ in the midst of them.

- We *can* have peace when deployment orders catch us by surprise.

- We *can* achieve equanimity when the new duty station is not what we wanted.

- Our mind does not have to fret when the doctor gives bad news or when our teenager is acting out.

Peace is a fruit of the spirit (Galatians 5:22). We have it. It just needs to be activated. I'm not an expert at dealing with stress. It still gets the best of me at times. Part of freedom's journey to bravery involves relying on the peace of Christ to overcome inner chaos.

How to Be Free from Inner Chaos:

1. **Acknowledge God's peace.** His peace is accessible to you. Ask God to grant you peace. He will.

2. **Cease striving.** Be still and know that God is bigger than what you are facing.

3. **Cultivate serenity by looking for joy.** Be grateful for the little things. In the midst of turmoil, there is always something to be thankful for. Birds singing, sunshine, warm coffee, a friend's hug, a child's laughter...

God wants us to be free from the bondage stress can create. God's peace that transcends all understanding is what sets us apart from the rest of the world. We can experience this precious gift of God. Not in our own strength but in God's.

How do you normally react to stress? What would happen if you first reached for God during stressful times? What practical step are you going to implement to cultivate equanimity?

Verses to Consider

And let the peace of Christ rule in your hearts, to which indeed you were called in one body. And be thankful. (Colossians 3:15)

You keep him in perfect peace whose mind is stayed on you, because he trusts in you. (Isaiah 26:3)

Do not be anxious about anything, but in everything by prayer and supplication with thanksgiving let your requests be made known to God. And the peace of God, which surpasses all understanding, will guard your hearts and your minds in Christ Jesus. What you have learned and received and heard and seen in me—practice these things, and the God of peace will be with you. (Philippians 4:6-7)

Prayer

Lord, thank you for showing us the way, for displaying perfect peace in the midst of a storm. I am grateful for your peace that transcends all understanding. Amen.

15

FREE FROM INTERFERENCE

by Muriel Gregory

I am a proud Navy brat. My dad served in the French Navy as a submariner. He was one of those crazy people who thought that it would be fun to live for 3 months in a "box" underneath the water. Since I am mildly claustrophobic, the sheer thought of it gives me a panic attack.

He finished his career on a nuclear submarine but started on a diesel submarine. He always laughingly said that there is nothing louder than a submarine diesel engine. I remember him sharing that his sleeping bunk was right on top of the engine. He had learned to sleep with the noise. It was the absence of that noise that would wake him up because it meant that something was wrong. I always found that amazing.

Even though I am not sure I could sleep next to a submarine's engine, I have to admit that I have become accustomed to many other noises in my life. Facebook, Twitter, Instagram, text messages, and instant notification of emails have drowned out God's voice. They have lured me to a state of spiritual sleep.

Sadly, I am also showing signs of withdrawal when the social media noise is absent. Here are some of my symptoms; maybe you can relate:

- I have an urge to check my phone when there is nothing going on.

- A feeling of low self-esteem will pop up when I do not get any likes on my post.

- Panic sets in when I drive through a cellular dead zone.

Do any of these ring true with you?

And he said, "Go out and stand on the mount before the Lord." And behold, the Lord passed by, and a great and strong wind tore the mountains and broke in pieces the rocks before the Lord, but the Lord was not in the wind. And after the wind an earthquake, but the Lord was not in the earthquake. And after the earthquake a fire, but the Lord was not in the fire. And after the fire the sound of a low whisper. And when Elijah heard it, he wrapped his face in his cloak and went out and stood at the entrance of the cave. And behold, there came a voice to him and said, "What are you doing here, Elijah?" (1 Kings 19:11-13 ESV)

Do you first reach out to your Facebook friends for advice or do you go to the Word of God? How often do you seek comfort in the likes you get from your Instagram post instead of the community of believers?

To hear God, we need to get rid of the noises of this world.

We get so used to those interferences that we no longer hear God's voice. Then we wonder why we face recurring problems and can't find the way out of difficult situations.

True freedom is found when we follow the Shepherd. The only way to follow the Shepherd is to hear his voice. "The thief comes only to steal and kill and destroy. I came that they may have life and have it abundantly" (John 10:10 ESV).

Abundant life! Who would reject that? Is it achievable? I wholeheartedly believe it is!

John Piper writes, "God is most glorified in us when we are most satisfied in him.[6]"

Abundant life starts when we tune in to God.

The more we get used to social noises, the less they look like interferences and the more they become the norm.

My dad could sleep on top of a diesel engine because it was the norm for him. I would have had the worst night ever, but here I am spiritually asleep on top of Facebook notifications and tweets from celebrities.

How to Be Free from Interference and Tune in to God:

1) **Discipline yourself:** Discipline is not a word we enjoy, yet a necessity in our Christian walk. When we accept Jesus as our Lord and Savior, we make the commitment to become his disciple. You cannot be a disciple without discipline.

2) **Choose a time and place:** There are plenty of things you do every day without thinking about them. Brushing your teeth, taking a shower, drinking coffee. Those actions are built into your routine and you accomplish them without much thought. Your quiet time with God will become a routine when you pick a regular time and place for it. Be regular and you will soon see the fruits.

3) **Make it a priority:** Choose God before you choose anything else. Open your Bible before picking up your phone. If it is not a priority, you will not stick with it.

---

[6] https://www.desiringgod.org/messages/god-is-most-glorified-in-us-when-we-are-most-satisfied-in-him

Verses to Consider

"Do you not know that in a race all runners run, but only one gets the prize? Run in such a way as to get the prize. Everyone who competes in the games goes into strict training. They do it to get a crown that will not lalst, but we do it to get a crown that will last forever. Therefore I do not run like someone running aimlessly; I do not fight like a boxer beating the air. No, I strike a blow to my body and make it my slave so that after I have preached to others, I myself will not be disqualified for the prize." (1 Corinthians 9:24-27)

"After he had dismissed them, he went up on a mountainside by himself to pray." (Matthew 14:23)

"Direct me in the path of your commands, for there I find delight. Turn my heart toward your statutes and not toward selfish gain. Turn my eyes away from worthless things; preserve my life according to your word." (Psalm 119:35-37)

Prayer

Lord, thank you for being a continuous presence in my life even when I am spiritually asleep. Help me to tune out the interferences of this world so I can hear your voice guiding me and letting me know that "this is the way, walk in it" (Isaiah 30:21). *Amen.*

16

FREE TO BE BRAVE

by Claudia Duff

I am free to be brave.

BRAVE is my personal word for this year. At first glance it looks quite glamorous, but as I dig a deeper, I'm uncovering some hard stuff under the surface.

Becoming brave is not the same as being brave.

There is a process that involves a daily struggle to take my thoughts captive and make them bend and yield to the things of God. I find I am my own worst enemy in my adventure of becoming brave. Trust me, *wanting* and *being* brave are not the same.

I've uncovered this freedom-giving truth in the book of Habakkuk, "God, the Lord, is my strength; he makes my feet like the deer's; he makes me tread on my high places" (Habakkuk 3:19).

According to the Word of God, the Lord *is* my strength, my bravery. He will walk me through places of trouble and suffering. Now, this is good news!

I can't make myself brave, only God can do that. Here's the good news: God has promised to accomplish his work in me. Despite my failings, God will be my strength and will make me brave even in times of trouble and suffering.

In preparation to begin focusing on my "one word," I picked up a book aptly named, *100 Days to Brave*. Perfect! I get to be brave and do it quickly. If you are also hoping for *instant brave* or a quick fix, we are both wrong. I am already planning to read this little book at least twice this year. . . possibly three times.

Brave ain't easy folks, not even a little bit.

You may be familiar with the Bible stories of "David and Goliath," "Daniel in the Lion's Den," and "Noah and the Ark." These guys were seriously brave, no doubt about it. Fortunately, I do not encounter giants or lions and have never experienced a flood that destroyed the entire earth.

This biblically epic kind of brave is not an option for me, or is it? My husband retired from active duty in 2013. Since then we've lived in five different homes, two states, and held multiple jobs between the two of us. I often feel like I am living in a lion's den of darkness as chaos devours my peace with sharp teeth. Financial responsibilities feel more like waves crashing over me. And I'm running out of stones to hurl at the giant uncertainties I face.

Bravery has never been so needed, yet felt so far out of my reach. But, I am determined to become *brave* and it will come with some effort on my part.

How to be Brave:

1. **Read.** Fuel your bravery by feeding your soul. In addition regularly meditating on God's Word, I also read my daily devotional and my book on being *brave*.

2. **Pray.** While reading, I find myself praying as the Spirit leads. Sometimes it's a prayer of gratitude, but mostly I talk to God about my concerns and ask for his help.

3. **Act.** I journal my prayers, thoughts, and an action point for each day. This is a simple way to apply God's wisdom and strength in the places I need to be brave.

Here's an excerpt from a recent journal entry: "When God said *all things*, he meant all things would work together for our good, to include the hard and prickly parts. I was made to be brave. How else would I be able to share my God-sized story with others? So, here I am chasing down *brave* like it owes me money, driving it like I stole it, and wearing it like a crown..."

My first action point for becoming *brave* was to accept and realize God wanted to work with what was present: me.

I didn't need to change so I could become brave; I needed to surrender myself and begin to allow the work of the Holy Spirit to make me brave.

Once again, the words of Habakkuk ring true, *"The Lord God is my strength, my bravery."*

Pursue the heart of God through a daily quiet time by reading verses on God's strength. Write your thoughts and prayers in a journal or share them aloud with a friend. There is no wrong way to spend time with God.

Just begin.

Verses to Consider

You shall not fear them, for it is the LORD your God who fights for you. (Deuteronomy 3:22)

Out of my distress I called on the Lord; the Lord answered me and set me free. The Lord is on my side; I will not fear. What can man do to me? (Psalm 118:5-6)

He fulfills the desire of those who fear him; he also hears their cry and saves them. (Psalm 145:19)

73

Prayer

Lord, thank you for being with me through thick and thin. Thank you for strengthening me and making me brave. You are wonderful and mighty. Amen.

17

FREE TO LIVE IN FREEDOM

by Claudia Duff

When I think of celebrating freedom my mind naturally slips to the 4th of July. Growing up in St. Louis, the 4Th of July was one of my favorite holidays. Celebrations included backyard barbeques, homemade ice cream, fireworks, music, and lots water flowing from hydrants (that's the old school way of keeping cool, no pools or waterparks).

It was like Christmas, only super-hot and loud. And sparklers. So, many sparklers! I was mesmerized by the lights and the fact someone allowed a little kid to play with fire! These are a few of the good times and great memories of the 4th from when I was a kid.

What about now? What does celebrating freedom look when it isn't a holiday? I admit freedom feels different now that I'm an adult. There is the realization that someone has to actually pay for the privilege of freedom—it's not free and it doesn't come cheap.

Women associated with the military have a deep understanding of that truth. We are either warriors ourselves, married to one, or raising one with a front row seat to the big show of freedom. And from our perspective, freedom is a lot more than a perk of life, it *is* life.

The Word of God declares both the gift of freedom and the responsibility of those who possess freedom.

Saints, there is work to be done to maintain freedom in Christ and also to spread the gospel to those who do not know the saving grace of Jesus. What are we doing to share our freedom in Christ?

We all know someone who is not free. Someone who has not met up the freedom fighter, Jesus. They are still in bondage and there is freedom to be grasped.

Heaven is a real place, but so is hell. Embracing freedom in Christ is not just to getting your "fire insurance" to avoid going to hell. Salvation sets us free to embrace a beautiful Savior who paid the eternal price for us to live in freedom beginning today. *As in right now!*

Freedom in Christ begins the moment you accept him. The moment you declare that Jesus is indeed Lord and Savior of your soul. We must tell of this freedom. God commands us to *"not submit again to a yoke of slavery"* (Galatians 5:1b).

How to Live in Christ's Freedom:

1. **Never forget your freedom**. The best way to live in freedom is to remember the cost of freedom and who paid it.

2. **Celebrate your salvation**. Keeping the power of salvation front and center in our lives will draw others to Christ.

3. **Talk like a free person**. If every part of our daily speech is permeated with the grateful knowledge that our freedom came from Christ, people will notice. They will notice it in our attitude and conversations. Are we being good ambassadors of Jesus, our freedom fighter? Can others see the freedom we have been granted? If not, why not? What do we need to throw off to embrace freedom in Christ with both hands?

Just as we celebrate the freedom of our nation on the 4th July, let's also truly celebrate the freedom only Christ can give every single day of our lives. Celebrate Jesus, our ultimate freedom fighter by sharing the Gospel with someone today.

Remember that your freedom was not free, but purchased through the power of the Cross, as you praise Jesus for this gift of freedom through salvation.

Verses to Consider

For God so loved the world, that he gave his only Son, that whoever believes in him should not perish but have eternal life. (John 3:16)

The thief comes only to steal and kill and destroy. I came that they may have life and have it abundantly. (John 10:10)

The work is great and widely spread, and we are separated on the wall, far from one another. In the place where you hear the sound of the trumpet, rally to us there. Our God will fight for us. (Nehemiah 4:19-20)

Prayer

Lord, let me shine your light of freedom. Help me to remember your sacrifice for our freedom as we appreciate the freedom of this country. Amen

FREE TO BE BRAVE

18

FREE TO REMOVE OUR MASKS

by Muriel Gregory

There I was again, scanning through my closet. The pressure to find the perfect outfit was intense. Should I wear a dress or pants, casual or dressy? Should I stick with neutral or go bohemian? We were being hailed at our new duty station. It was not our first hail and farewell but it was our first impression to this new unit.

I wanted it to be perfect.

We strive for perfection to hide our flaws and escape evaluations. From hosting people in our homes to excelling on the job, we often feel the pressure to perform well. We are Pinterest gals living in a image-driven world.

Social media creates a distorted view of life. Since only the good stuff is posted, we only see the best moments in the lives of those around us. The spotless house, the creative birthday cake, the fun vacation, the flawless body, the beautiful children, etc. We fill our Pinterest boards with a perfect life, but the reality is often opposite.

We seek to achieve perfection because we fear criticism. So we close our doors to hide the mess. We close our hearts to cover the pain of a less-than-ideal marriage and challenges with children.

And we wear a mask--*the perfect mask.* This mask answers, "I'm fine" when asked how we're doing. This mask smiles even though tears are about to burst. Our mask hides the imperfections and flaws, keeping criticism, rejection, and judgment at bay.

This mask, however, shackles our hearts and blocks the freedom that Christ provides. As long as we wear the mask, we will not experience freedom.

You therefore must be perfect, as your heavenly Father is perfect. (Matthew 5:48)

We see *perfect* as flawless and immaculate, but the Greeks defined this word as mature and complete. In this verse, *perfect* means genuine, complete, and mature.

Being genuine means bravely removing the mask with the courage to let our flaws be seen. We will never be free if we are not truly being ourselves.

How to Be Free from Our Masks:

1. **Reflect on God.** Psalm 19:7. God is perfect and his law is perfect. The more we reflect on his truth, the more we rely on his provision.

2. **Abide in him.** 1 John 4:17. When we abide in Christ our love grows more complete.

3. **Never give up.** Philippians 3:12-15. Forget about the past, the mistakes, the masks and focus on the prize that Jesus has set before us. He calls you his own and invites you into freedom.

4. **Be renewed.** Romans 12:2. Transformation starts in your mind. As you reflect on God, abide in Christ, and strive for the prize, you will be changed from the inside out.

I am not bound to win, I am bound to be true. I am not bound to succeed, but I live up to the light that I have in Christ.

As a recovering perfectionist, one of the tools that helped me the most was redefining perfection. I may not be a perfect person but I will resolve to be an impeccable one. Impeccable simply means not liable to sin. Even though I fall short at times, my freedom goal is to glorify God and not be conformed to the world.

- I can be impeccable, when I live by the promise that Christ died for me (Romans 10:13).

- I can be impeccable, when I choose a life of obedience over fake perfection (John 14:12).

- I am free to be brave when I choose to conform to God's will, rather than follow the ways of the world (Romans 12:2).

What mask are you wearing? Spend some time looking at areas of your life where perfectionism holds you captive. Ask God to show you areas that you won't allow yourself to be less than perfect. Write them down. Share them with a friend or two to hold you accountable.

Verses to Consider

Him we proclaim, warning everyone and teaching everyone with all wisdom, that we may present everyone mature in Christ. (Colossians 1:28)

Epaphras, who is one of you, a servant of Christ Jesus, greets you, always struggling on your behalf in his prayers, that you may stand mature and fully assured in all the will of God. (Colossians 4:12)

And let steadfastness have its full effect, that you may be perfect and complete, lacking in nothing. (James 1:4)

Prayer

Lord, I am truly thankful for the gift of your son. I am thankful for the work that was done on the cross that allows me to live an impeccable life, free from sin. Amen.

19

FREE TO BE AUTHENTIC

by Adrienne Terrebonne

Ever struggle to be free from worrying about what other people think?

Did you know people-pleasing is actually a sin? Galatians tells us: "Am I now trying to win the approval of human beings or of God? Or am I trying to please people? If I were still trying to please people, I would not be a servant of Christ" (Galatians 1:10 NASB).

Ouch.

I've been a people-pleaser my whole life. As a first-born, I've always wanted to do the right things and make the best choices so that others would accept me. Growing up, I struggled to find the right fit of friends. I tended to change my identity based on the people I was hanging out with at the time.

After marrying my husband, the Air Force took us many different places, and again I found myself struggling to discover my true identity. I wanted to fit in with my Bible study girls but I also wanted to hang out at the club on base with other friends. The inner conflict was real as I attempted to discover exactly who God made me to be.

My husband changed career fields after twelve years of flying bombers. Although he remained in the USAF, this career change took us to an army post where I was exposed to many different people and ideas.

We began attending a church in our new town. This church felt different to us. Church leadership encouraged authenticity, and for the first time in my life, I learned what it meant to be real.

I learned how to expose my struggles, hurts, and disappointments to others instead of hiding behind a mask of perfection.

It was in this loving church family that I came to know Jesus more intimately, and I developed friendships with others who were struggling with similar issues.

I learned to be authentic instead of trying to say all the right things so people would like me. 2 Corinthians 3:17 reminds me that I am free from the pressure of the opinions of others: *Now the Lord is the Spirit, and where the Spirit of the Lord is, there is freedom.* (NIV)

When we are filled with the Holy Spirit, and when we worship in a place with other people who are being led by the Holy Spirit, authenticity comes naturally. It is a natural product of the Spirit giving freedom and grace.

When I choose to be brave, I discover the freedom to allow others to see my weakness.

I'm not suggesting you tell everyone your deepest, darkest secrets. And don't get me wrong—it isn't always easy to expose my struggles. I still fall prey to people-pleasing, hoping others will like me. But when we follow the Holy Spirit, he will show us how to be authentic.

How to Be Authentic:

1. **Study the Bible.** In order to know who we are, we need to read God's love letter to us. When we are secure in his love, we're more likely to be authentic, seeking only his approval.

84

2. **Find a church home.** I encourage you to find a church with leadership who is not afraid of authenticity. And go further by joining a small group where you can find even deeper community.

3. **Go first.** Sometimes all it takes is for one person to open up about their struggles.

During one of our many moves, I struggled to connect with others, even in our small group. One Sunday, my husband and I shared our emotional battle with infertility, and the floodgates opened. Women came to me afterward, wrapping their arms around me, promising to pray for our situation. Others invited me to meet for coffee. These women are still some of my dearest friends, and it all started when we told our story.

When you struggle with your self-worth, meditate on the truth found in God's Word. Specifically, read Psalm 139.

This week, invite a good friend to do something together and "go first." Be brave as you open up by sharing a struggle or concern with her and watch how authenticity grows your relationship even deeper.

Friend, you are God's masterpiece. He loves you and wants you to be the person he made you to be. Cast aside the tendency to please others and instead live your life in the freedom of the Holy Spirit.

Verses to Consider

For we are his workmanship, created in Christ Jesus for good works, which God prepared beforehand, that we should walk in them. (Ephesians 2:10)

Many are the women of proven worth, but you have excelled them all. Charm is deceptive and beauty fleeting; the woman who fears the LORD is to be praised. (Proverbs 31:29-30 NASB)

Two are better than one, because they have a good reward for their toil. For if they fall, one will lift up his fellow. But woe to him who is alone when he falls and has not another to lift him up! (Ecclesiastes 4:9-10)

Prayer

Lord, thank you for the truth of Scripture. Show me who I am according to your Word and bless me with courage to be authentic with those whom you place in my life. Amen.

20

FREE TO SPEAK

by Kori Yates

Say something.

"I don't know enough to share Jesus." I've heard these words many times before, even sometimes from myself. I have moments when I question my authority on subjects and wonder if someone will ask questions I can't answer.

What if they have problems I don't know how to fix? What if they ask me where a verse or topic is found in the Bible? What if I stutter and "um" my way through the whole conversation? A million questions run through my brain and there is only one answer to them all.

His name is Jesus.

We could come up with a million reasons why we don't share Jesus with our neighbor, our friend, the lady at the commissary, or the new family in the unit. A million reasons that at the end of the day are simply excuses.

Yet in Christ, I am free to speak.

Just a few weeks ago my ten-year-old son brought this realization back to me. It was youth Sunday at our post chapel so the kids helped with the service. From ushering to playing the piano, kids volunteered for everything except the preaching. The adults were fine with the Chaplain giving the message. Apparently, my ten-year-old, shy, introverted little man felt the Lord give him a push.

He immediately volunteered to share a message. Truth? It scared the tar out of me! I imagined him getting up in front of everyone and saying absolutely nothing. I doubted he could have an actual plan in place that he followed for a sermon. My husband and I prayed about it and prayed with him. My husband, my son, and I chatted with a local Chaplain friend as well as a pastor friend back home.

We asked my son if he had specific Bible passage on his mind - he did. We helped him prepare by brainstorming what he learned from the Scripture and how to share his point with others. We printed it out and practiced his remarks, and then we printed an extra copy for my husband in the event the little man froze.

We got to the chapel for youth Sunday and little man wasn't nervous at all. He was excited! When the time came, he stepped up on his stool behind the pulpit and spoke the truth, not missing a point on his notes. From reading the verse to telling personal stories, he talked for about fifteen minutes. I was amazed.

I saw Jesus in the bravery of my ten-year-old son.

What God reminded me that day was that we are all free to speak about Jesus. If we have the Holy Spirit living inside of us, we have a story and a Savior to share. We don't know all the answers, but we do know the One who does.

Go therefore and make disciples of all nations, baptizing them in the name of the Father and of the Son and of the Holy Spirit, teaching them to observe all that I have commanded you. And behold, I am with you always, to the end of the age. (Matthew 28:19-20)

Jesus commanded us to speak, to make disciples, and to teach. he didn't caveat that with "after you attend seminary" or "once you study your Bible for a few years" or "when you can name the books of the Bible in order." There were no caveats.

Is it important to study? Is it important to use the Word of God correctly? Absolutely. But the story we all have to share is what Jesus has done in us. We all have something to say.

How to Speak:

1. **Jesus:** Is Jesus your Savior? This is key. If you don't know him, it's super hard to share him. If you've never met Jesus, we would love to share with you! You can message us on social media or send us an email (info@plantingroots.net)!

2. **Think:** What difference has Jesus made in you? What has Jesus taught you through his Word and through others? These are just a couple of questions to ponder because they are the exact things you can share with someone else.

3. **Expect:** God so many times brings someone in our paths that needs us to say something. Sometimes they have similar experiences to ours or they may need encouragement for the day. Others may be searching for the truth, life, and hope that we have already found. Go looking for what God is doing around you.

4. **Speak:** When God gives you the nudge, just speak. If you don't know answers, just tell them you'll find out and then get back to them. Remember, you're not expected to know everything, but you do know the One who does. And perfection is not his aim, obedience is. BE BRAVE!

What difference Jesus has made in you? What He has taught you? You have something to say. Pray that the Lord would bring someone in your path this week, then pray for courage to speak.

Verses to Consider

For I am not ashamed of the gospel, for it is the power of God for salvation to everyone who believes, to the Jew first and also to the Greek. (Romans 1:16)

Oh give thanks to the Lord; call upon his name; make known his deeds among the peoples! (Psalm 105:1)

Of this gospel I was made a minister according to the gift of God's grace, which was given me by the working of his power. To me, though I am the very least of all the saints, this grace was given, to preach to the Gentiles of the unsearchable riches of Christ, and to bring to light for everyone what is the plan of the mystery hidden for ages in God, who created all things. (Ephesians 3:7-9)

Prayer

Lord, help me to know those with whom you'd have me speak. Help me to hear your voice to go, and then give me the courage to be obedient. I can't wait to see how you use me! Amen.

21

FREE TO COLOR WELL

by Kori Yates

Freedom requires boundaries.

In first grade, coloring was important. It was a developmental skill that was necessary for many reasons, but for me it was one of my favorite parts of school, coloring and recess. I felt like coloring was a special skill I possessed—until I met this *one* other boy in my class.

Truly, I could color a lovely picture, but he was phenomenal. Pressing hard on the crayon, he colored with bold dark strokes which made the colors stand out brilliantly, covering every white spot on the picture. Once he filled in the color, he would go back with a black crayon and color all the lines in a thick, dark black.

I was amazed at his coloring. My picture looked nice, but his was awesome. Coloring in the lines carried a whole different meaning after looking at his pictures.

Crazy as it is, I learned some God-lessons from that memory. First, God draws the lines in my life and gives me a chance to do the coloring. Second, simply staying in the lines (following accepted morals) is not enough. Third, the beautiful lines and strong colors mean the world sees Jesus in me more.

Bottom line: the lines are good.

As Christians, we have been set free, but that doesn't mean it's a "free for all."

God sets boundaries to freedom both for our good and for his glory. As Peter points out, our freedom is not a covering for evil but an opportunity to "silence the ignorance of foolish men." There is an expectation to stay in the lines and to do it well, not to blur the lines or color so lightly that no one can even tell if we colored at all.

For such is the will of God that by doing right you may silence the ignorance of foolish men. Act as free men, and do not use your freedom as a covering for evil but use it as bondslaves of God. (1 Peter 2:15-16 NASB)

Coloring well does not always come easily, but we serve a God of grace. I want to only do what he has called me to, no more and no less. And I want to do it well.

Those light colors? We can go back over them again and again, making them brilliant hues. We can make the lines clearer should we need to. I think too that some of that crayon is erasable and God's grace truly covers those places I've where the lines are messy.

Our lives are meant to be a beautiful picture of Christ.

I long to color well and to finish life with a brilliantly colored picture of Jesus.

How to Color Well:

1. **Love Jesus more** than anything else. Remembering what he has done both in our personal lives and throughout history will bring us to a place of gratitude and love where we cannot help but want to color.

2. **Don't compare yourself to others.** As women, we tend to play the comparison game . . . a lot. Our lives should be

compared only to the standard of righteousness, not to anything of the world. It's not my picture against yours, it's mine against Jesus's. Thankfully, we serve a God of grace and mercy, but our desire should be to color well.

3. **Embrace the lines.** Whether free spirit or square, our pictures turn out best when we follow his plan.

4. **Encourage others.** We all have a picture God has designed us to color, one that shows the world who he is. Encourage others to color well.

This week, feel free to color. Recognize God's boundaries as blessings. What has he asked of you and what has he said no to? Some areas are definitive for all of us, but we all have different callings on our lives. Color yours well.

If you're unsure, just ask. Jesus is faithful and will show you areas where you might have stepped out a bit or areas you need to cover with color. Follow him.

Verses to Consider

The Lord is my chosen portion and my cup; you hold my lot. The lines have fallen for me in pleasant places; indeed, I have a beautiful inheritance. I bless the Lord who gives me counsel; in the night also my heart instructs me. I have set the Lord always before me; because he is at my right hand, I shall not be shaken. Therefore my heart is glad, and my whole being rejoices; my flesh also dwells secure. (Psalm 16:5-9)

We will not compare ourselves with each other as if one of us were better and another worse. We have far more interesting things to do with our lives. Each one of us is an original. (Galatians 5:26 MSG)

Therefore be imitators of God, as beloved children. And walk in love, as Christ loved us and gave himself up for us, a fragrant offering and sacrifice to God. But sexual immorality and all impurity or covetousness must not even be named among you, as is proper among saints. Let there be no filthiness nor foolish talk nor crude joking, which are out of place, but instead let there be thanksgiving. (Ephesians 5:1-4)

Prayer

Lord, I long for my life to be a beautiful picture of your image displayed through me. Help me to go when you say go and stop when you say stop. Use my life to draw others to you. Amen.

22

FREE TO CRY

by Kristin Goodrich

"Toughen up, buttercup!"

"Put on your big girl panties!"

"No tears. Nope."

Military culture projects an eleventh commandment to women in uniform: *Thou shalt not cry.*

I spent my formative young adult years cultivating military professionalism *in spite of* being a woman. I swung hard toward leadership and excellence. I felt as though I didn't have any time to deal with my emotions, lest I be taunted about "that time of the month." In recent years, I've worked at developing my feminine side in emotionally intense situations, knowing that the Lord delights in me as a *Christian—military—woman!*

I am starting to figure out what to do with my tears.

I enjoy taking personality and aptitude tests, and the results always give me insight on how God has made me unique: "I praise you, for I am fearfully and wonderfully made" (Psalm 139:14a).

My strengths cluster in executive function and strategic thinking, which I easily apply to my faith journey as well as my military lifestyle.

In my Christian walk, I have been reading through the Bible for years now. I pour through books covering history, biography, principles and practices for leadership, fiction, and much more. Many, but not all, include components of a Christian worldview.

While wearing a uniform, I absorbed the lessons I was taught and the behaviors I saw modeled. My voice is now deeper and can authoritatively carry quite some distance. Through my facial expressions, I can express disapproval as well as an expectation of excellence. I lean into the challenges of military life and work.

In my pursuit of growth, my aptitudes have easily been applied to growing deeper in relationship with the Lord while also finding my niche within the military community long after exchanging my active-duty ID for a dependent (now retiree) ID card.

However, I have only just recently begun to focus on the third way that the Lord has created me as a Christian military woman. Conflicting opinions abound regarding women in uniform, as well as how women in the military community "should" behave. Yet, God created us all with purpose—male *and* female.

I like my casual clothes, wash-and-wear haircut, and my forthright personality. But I also like that the Lord is taking me on a journey to embrace the "woman" in my story.

I'm learning grace can demonstrate strength.

I'm pushing through the confusion I feel as I identify and label various emotions, which often lead to tears.

A decade ago, I gave my friend Margaret, a fellow Air Force wife, permission to completely revamp my wardrobe. To this day, I make mindful choices about colors and styles that suit me more than others.

I've started wearing my Naval Academy class ring, accepting that some will be instantly put off by the "cocky, ring-knocker" visual. I love that my ring is inscribed with my name and a reference to Psalm 139. Every one of the twenty-four verses in that Psalm are rich and deep. They have been a comfort to me for more than thirty years.

I have focused on improving areas that don't come naturally. I am starting to figure out that tears come in all shapes and sizes, just like we do. And sometimes my tears are mixed in with laughter and joy.

Six months ago, I began taking basic classical ballet classes, and I will continue to go to classes twice a week this upcoming year. I am being evermore intentional in softening my voice and affirming the strengths and successes of others. And most profoundly for me, I let others see my eyes well up with tears and hear my voice fill up with emotion.

How to Be Free to Cry:

So, how do we become "Free to Cry" as Christian military women seeking to be brave?

1. **Embrace your strengths**, knowing that the Lord has made you wonderful (Psalm 139:14a).

2. **Accept that your complexities are part of who you are**, whether or not you and I are similar or vastly different! Emotional strength in a woman can be so attractive.

3. **Spend time and effort depending on the Lord** as you exercise the weaker or less confident areas in your life.

4. **Read all twenty-four verses of Psalm 139** and pick one verse to reflect on this week.

Every time you re-read Psalm 139, find a new truth to remember, a new challenge to consider, and a new blessing to celebrate. You *are* fearfully and wonderfully made...even during a public, ugly cry.

Verses to Consider

O Lord, you have searched me and known me! (Psalm 139:1)

Where shall I go from your Spirit? Or where shall I flee from your presence. (Psalm 139:7)

How precious to me are your thoughts, O God! How vast is the sum of them! (Psalm 139:17)

Search me, O God, and know my heart! Try me and know my thoughts! And see if there be any grievous way in me, and lead me in the way everlasting! (Psalm 139:23-24)

Prayer

Lord, I can be challenged to grow in any, or all, three categories you've been leading me in as a Christian—military— woman. Help me to celebrate growth in each area. Amen.

23

FREE TO TRUST GOD

by Katye Riselli

I stared at the names, crestfallen. Those weren't the teachers we wanted. It felt a bit like a gut punch, and all too quickly I was criticizing myself and the route I'd chosen in this motherhood moment: "So much for just praying about it - I should have emailed the school. "

I found myself half praying again, half working through my disappointment and searching for resolution:

God, I thought I asked you to give them the best teachers? I wish I knew the school's process for placing kids, if I knew that they specifically matched each girl with the teacher that would be best for them, maybe this would be ok. I wonder if I should call the principal?

But as I wrestled, I began to see the irony of my own temper tantrum with God. I had asked him to place my girls with the best teachers, but in this moment of disappointment, I didn't trust he had. If I believed the principal and last year's teachers knew my girls well enough to appropriately place them, how could I not trust God knew them better?

The truth is, as much as I say I trust God, I still want control.

I'm hardwired to plan, organize, and orchestrate. And in most areas of my life, especially as a military wife and mom, my ability to make a plan, adapt a plan, and execute a plan feels like a job requirement.

But when it comes to walking by faith, my natural inclination to direct all things needs to take a backseat. The control I crave is an illusion that will never satisfy. My white-knuckled grip merely reveals my need to trust.

As a mother, it's hard to let go, to lift my eyes from the challenge of the moment. But as a woman of faith, I'm not called to blind trust in an abstract God. I'm free to trust a personal God who cares about what I care about and who sees more clearly than I do.

Psalm 139 reminds me that God knew my girls before I did. He knit them together in my womb, he saw them before I did, he knows all their days already. He knows better than I do what they need – in school, in friends, in confidence, in all the ways I prayed for this upcoming school year, he knows.

Remembering who I trust reminds me how many times he has proven trustworthy. There have been so many times that I didn't have the answers as a mother: why one baby couldn't eat, or why a toddler couldn't use her legs. By faith I sought the Lord who created them and entrusted their healing to him. Today both girls are thriving with no outward signs of those early challenges.

God's faithful provision in the times I couldn't control the outcome frees me to trust him with my girls in the moments that I want to direct their steps.

I can release my grip because God isn't letting go.

How to Be Free to Trust:

1. **Remember who you trust.** Who do you trust? In your ability or your experience? Who do you turn to when you feel life is out of control? Consider reminding

yourself, "I know whom I have believed, and am convinced that he is able to guard what I have entrusted to him until that day" (2 Timothy 1:12b).

2. **Recall God's provision.** When has the Lord provided for you? How has the Lord been faithful to you? "The eyes of all look to you and you give them their food at the proper time. You open your hand and satisfy the desires of every living thing" (Psalm 145:15-16).

3. **Release your grip.** What are you holding on to? What area of life beckons you to trust God? Picture yourself securely placing whatever it is into the Lord's hand. Whenever you're inclined to snatch it back, fix your eyes on Jesus (not the challenge, not your fear, not the what-if scenario). He is the author and perfector of faith.

4. **Remain in God's love.** Do you ever find yourself trying to DO something? Or do you seek distraction (even in good things, like a book) rather than just being still? When you're practicing trust, resist the urge to walk away, even when you are discouraged. When you feel like it's up to you to *do* something, resist the lie and focus on where you need to *be*. He is the source of your trust. He will strengthen you so that you do not grow weary and lose heart.

Trusting God isn't just something I do and check off my list as accomplished. To live in trust requires remaining *with* the One who counters my natural desire to control with his supernatural ability to love.

God is the source of my trust. When I remain in him, my life – my motherhood – reflects the fruit of that relationship. My greatest accomplishments will not be what I *do*, but where I choose to *be*.

Verses to Consider

I am the true vine, and my Father is the gardener. . . Remain in me, as I also remain in you. No branch can bear fruit by itself; it must remain in the vine. Neither can you bear fruit unless you remain in me. (John 15:1-5 NIV)

Therefore, since we are surrounded by such a great cloud of witnesses, let us throw off everything that hinders and the sin that so easily entangles. And let us run with perseverance the race marked out for us, fixing our eyes on Jesus, the author and perfector of faith. For the joy set before him he endured the cross, scorning its shame, and sat down at the right hand of the throne of God. Consider him who endured such opposition from sinners, so that you will not grow weary and lose heart. (Hebrews 12:1-3 NIV)

Prayer

Lord, remind me of your faithfulness and give me eyes to see your provision in the circumstances. I long to control the outcome rather than trust you. I surrender my desire to DO and direct, and I ask for grace to BE, content and confident in you. Amen.

24

FREE TO BE A GIANT OF FAITH

by Kori Yates

I feel stuck.

I want to be strong and mighty, a faithful, mature child of the King. Yet, I seem to struggle with the same things over and over. Reading my Bible, attending church, spending time in prayer, and building community with other believers are all things I do regularly.

Really, I do.

And yet, sometimes I still feel stuck. I feel like I am a twig of a tree, a sapling, instead of being the huge, strong, mature tree I long to be.

Tripping over the same traps, I tell myself, "This time will be different." But then I allow fear and anxiety seep into my heart, hoping nobody notices that I am such a weak little sapling. Seasons like PCSing, deployments, and retirement discussions can bring on these feelings, but so can the everyday commitments, jobs, children, and the ever-changing community in which we live.

I want to be free from the constraints of my knowledge and understanding and reach far beyond into the knowledge of God.

They will be like a tree planted by the water that sends out its roots by the stream. It does not fear when heat comes; its leaves are always green. It has no worries in a year of drought and never fails to bear fruit. (Jeremiah 17:8 NIV)

When Billy Graham passed away, countless interviews and discussions about his life showcased a giant in the faith. We read about giants in Scripture like Paul, Nehemiah, Mary, and Deborah.

Rarely, in glimpses of their lives, do we see fear, anxiety, uncertainty, or doubt.

I want to grow myself, change myself, help myself. There are things I can do to facilitate growth like Scripture reading and time in prayer. But at the end of the day, God brings the growth.

Looking at my own life and heart, I wonder if I'll ever come close to the example of spiritual giants. In the pondering, though, God reminds me of two things.

- **The Christian walk is not like Facebook.** I measure the everyday feelings of my heart and thoughts of my mind to the intermittent public actions of others. That is not how God measures at all.

A legacy of faithfulness comes from perseverance, not perfection.

- **I don't grow myself.** It is my nature to fix things. I want to fix everything from the challenges my family is facing to the struggle of a stranger in the grocery store. The thing I want to fix most is often myself.

Look back at Jeremiah 17:7, "But blessed is the one who trusts in the Lord, whose confidence is in him" (NIV). Those who trust in the Lord, who have confidence in him—those people will be like a tree. Surely, we can do that.

How to Become a Giant of Faith:

1. **Remember:** Make a list of what he has already done, run through your mind evidence of his faithfulness— everything from homes in new places to lifelong battle buddies and from regular paychecks to government shutdowns. We need to remember his faithfulness.

2. **Build Relationship:** We cannot grow ourselves but we can build a relationship with the Lord. As in every relationship, communication goes two ways. It takes time and intentional effort. Spend time with the Lord. Talk to him, listen to him, read the Bible, join with fellow believers in worship and life.

3. **Rest:** Trust that God is doing a work in you and rest. In our striving to do it all right and be enough for everyone, we have to be reminded that we are never enough…but he is. Rest in God's will, way, and timing.

4. **Trust:** We may never see the results of all God has done in us, the full picture, but it doesn't mean he hasn't used us. We may never see the legacy we leave. But if we are obedient, our legacy will be one of Jesus.

Remember how you used to live and who you are now. The difference in the two is Jesus. He is growing you. What is one way God has been strengthening you lately?

Spend time with God this week, learning and listening. Seek him in the day-to-day and watch as he changes your heart and perspective. Rest in him. We will never measure up or think we have "made it." Our hope is in the extraordinary things God can do with an ordinary life. How can resting in faith make your current challenge look different?

Verses to Consider

But the seed in the good soil, these are the ones who have heard the word in an honest and good heart, and hold it fast, and bear fruit with perseverance. (Romans 8:15 NASB)

I planted, Apollos watered, but God was causing the growth. So then neither the one who plants nor the one who waters is anything, but God who causes the growth.
(1 Corinthians 3:5-6 NASB)

Prayer

Lord, help me to trust you today. Give me confidence in who you are and what you have done so I can step forward in courage as you grow me into the courageous person I long to be. Amen.

I wrote this poem a few years ago as we launched **Planting Roots** in 2014. These thoughts are still the desire of my heart.

I long to be a tree

strong and brave and tall,

to live the life that God intended.

Answering the call,

I want to grow from a stick

to a huge and mighty tree,

with roots deep in the soil

of what he's done for me.

Soaking up the hope and life

only he could give

into a trunk of God himself

that is the strength to live.

Leading, guiding, restoring

he grows me stronger still.

With arms raised in worship

because of hope fulfilled,

reaching out into the world.

bearing fruit wherever I go,

I become the mighty tree

I wished for so long ago.

He sees in me that mighty tree

that only he could grow.

He builds me step by step,

this I surely know.

I worship him this day,

not because of who I am,

but because of what he can do in me--

and it's in that hope I stand.

May he be glorified

in the tree I grow to be,

a testament to the world

of what he is to me.

25

FREE TO EXHALE

by Sarah McKinney

I didn't even realize I had been holding my breath.

Wandering through my days with a "fake it till you make it" mentality had created a burning in my chest and a panic in my heart. I needed to release the tension, but how do I breathe easy when I'm not sure of the road before me? Maybe you've felt the need for the "fresh air" of courage and hope in your military experience as well.

- Waiting for news of the next assignment...we hold our breath.

- Waiting on that promotion board decision...we hold our breath.

- Waiting on that referral we desperately need for our child...we hold our breath.

Too often there are more unknowns than we can count, and the stability we may crave can be even hard to come by. I get it. *I'm living it.* But we can't just keep holding our breath, afraid of what the future will bring.

I'm discovering a better way to release the tension: "Come to me, all you who are weary and burdened, and I will give you rest. Take my yoke upon you and learn from me, for I am gentle and humble in heart, and you will find rest for your souls" (Matthew 11:28-29 NIV).

Yes, there really is freedom from worry. His name is Jesus. His gentle and humble heart sees you (and me) struggling to bear up under the weight of all the worries and trials of this life and he offers something better.

Jesus offers himself.

This is where the exhale is possible. *This* is where your shoulders come down and your chest rises up to enter peace. Rest, peace, and breathing out a sigh of relief (exhale) doesn't come because your problems magically disappeared or were instantly solved. Nope. The ability to exhale isn't actually circumstantial.

We exhale because we are fully convinced that there is NOTHING in our lives that is bigger than the GOD who holds our hearts.

We release our breath not because our situation is easy or even solved. Letting go of stress, we choose to remember that we are loved more deeply than we can imagine. Exhale and lean in to the truth that Jesus really is who he says he is. We are free to be brave as we choose to believe his promises never, ever fail.

Not ever.

Truth is, we may not get the answers we were hoping for. That promotion board or assignment list may herald news that we would still rather not hear. But still, we can exhale. We can look into the eyes of Jesus, who has promised to complete the good work he started in you (and in me). He is faithful to complete his work!

How to Release Your Fears and Exhale:

1. **Bring your worry to the Lord.** Uproot the reason you're holding your breath and name it.

2. **Search out verses that reference the character of God.** This is a practice that a mentor challenged me to try years ago, and it has changed my life. I can testify that you can't be saturated with the character of God and still be afraid.

3. **Submit your concern into the Presence and Truth of who he is in prayer.** Pray about your concerns in view of his character. There is such freedom found in looking at your worries through the lens of who he is.

4. **Release your expectation for a certain result.** For some (including me) this can be the hardest part. Trust him to do what is best. There is no one on this planet that loves you more than he does. He sees all of you, your past, your present and your future. He is trustworthy to hold that which you hold most dear: "Return to your rest, my soul, for the LORD has been good to you" (Psalm 116:7 NIV).

Read that last verse again. Remind yourself of who he is and his great love for you and... exhale. I am doing it, too. May you find sweet rest as you abide in Jesus…the Author and Completer of your faith.

Verses to Consider

For God alone, O my soul, wait in silence, for my hope is from him. He only is my rock and my salvation, my fortress; I shall not be shaken. On God rests my salvation and my glory; my mighty rock, my refuge is God. Trust in him at all times, O people; pour out your heart before him; God is a refuge for us. (Psalm 62:5-8)

Therefore I tell you, do not worry about your life, what you will eat or drink; or about your body, what you will wear. Is not life more than food, and the body more than clothes? Look at the birds of the air; they do not sow or reap or store away in barns, and yet your heavenly Father feeds them. Are you not much more valuable than they? Can any one of you by worrying add a single hour to your life?

'And why do you worry about clothes? See how the flowers of the field grow. They do not labor or spin. Yet I tell you that not even Solomon in all his splendor was dressed like one of these.

If that is how God clothes the grass of the field, which is here today and tomorrow is thrown into the fire, will he not much more clothe you—you of little faith? So do not worry, saying, 'What shall we eat?' or 'What shall we drink?' or 'What shall we wear?' For the pagans run after all these things, and your heavenly Father knows that you need them.
(Matthew 6:25-32 NIV)

Prayer

Lord, I confess that I get easily tangled up in the worries and trials of my life. I know that you do not want me to obsess about my future or the things that I have no control over. With courage born of faith, I release my concerns to you as I exhale with freedom from worry. Amen.

26

FREE TO BREATHE

by Kori Yates

Anxiety. Fear. Two feelings we battle whether we like it or not.

New places and faces. Sending children off to school. New jobs. New bosses. Unknown futures. Boards, battles, and buddies. Fear and anxiety can come with them all if we let them.

Living overseas for the last couple of years, I have seen it first-hand a bit more often. We live a bit closer to each other as neighbors and there aren't quite as many of us, so these stairwells can truly show our true colors. Add that to living in a foreign country, still sending folks on deployments, watching children head off to other continents on their own, watching family members struggle with things we are too far away to help, and you have some anxious and fearful moments that could easily turn to days, weeks, or months if we let them.

But God.

Those words start everything in a new direction. They give hope in the darkest of places and joy in the strangest of times.

God has a better plan than living in fear or anxiety.

He tells us about the life he offers in John 10:10: "The thief comes only to steal and kill and destroy; I have come that they may have life, and have it to the full."

How do we leave the fear and anxiety behind and step into the abundance and joy of Christ? It's a day-by-day and sometimes moment-by-moment effort.

But God.

I know you breathe involuntarily every day, but I want you to breathe on purpose today.

Breathe in—fill your lungs with the hope and the peace that comes from God alone. Breathe out—expel all that is not of him.

A friend of mine used to do this exercise frequently for a Bible study I attended. As the large group started, she would lead us to breathe in the things of God and breathe out the rest. I know it's just a breathing exercise, but it was amazing to me how taking the time to stop and breathe made a difference in my whole morning.

So today, in the mess, anxiousness, fear, crazy of this moment, I want to challenge you to do the same. Feel FREE to BREATHE, my friends.

How to Breathe:
1. **Stop:** Take a timeout. Stop what you're doing for just a moment.
2. **Change:** Change environments, whether that means stepping outside, to another room, or driving in the car.
3. **Focus:** Not on circumstance or situations, but on Jesus. Saying Scripture in your head or out loud is a great way to do this.
4. **Breathe:** Breathe deep. Slow your heart rate down a bit and focus on filling your lungs as you breathe in the hope, joy and peace of God.

Take at least one moment today to breathe, to step away from the messy and mundane and breathe the things of God again. You'll be amazed at the difference it makes.

Verses to Consider

Since then, you have been raised with Christ, set your hearts on things above, where Christ is, seated at the right hand of God. Set your minds on things above, not on earthly things.
(Colossians 3:1-2)

Rejoice in the Lord always; again I will say, Rejoice. Let your reasonableness be known to everyone. The Lord is at hand; do not be anxious about anything, but in everything by prayer and supplication with thanksgiving let your requests be made known to God. And the peace of God, which surpasses all understanding, will guard your hearts and minds in Christ Jesus. Finally, brothers, whatever is honorable, whatever is just, whatever is pure, whatever is lovely, whatever is commendable, if there is any excellence, if there is anything worthy of praise, thing about these things. What you have learned and received and heard and seen in me – practice these things, and the God of peace will be with you. (Philippians 4:4-9)

Prayer

Lord, help me breathe today, to find moments to step away from circumstances for just a second and breathe in you again. Amen

27

FREE TO JUMP

by Kori Yates

What is one thing that burns in your heart to do? A passion that just won't let you go?

Have you ever had such a desire of your heart? Surely, we all have. They come at interesting moments when we least expect them and usually make us feel wholly unqualified and just a bit scared.

I had one of those moments when I decided to join the Marine Corps. At the ripe old age of 31, I wasn't in the majority of recruits the Corps accept. I even required a waiver just for them to let me in, but I knew I was supposed to be there for some crazy reason. About a week before my first day in the Marine Corps, I had started to question quitting my job, putting my possessions in storage, and making the cross-country trek. I was a bit intimidated.

Showing up and running through that first week, I wondered whether I was truly qualified to be in Marine training. Everything hurt. I wasn't as fast as some, didn't score as high as some on obstacles and leadership scenarios, and trying to stay awake in class was no joke! I questioned whether I should be there at all. Was I really cut out for this?

Did I really have what it takes? Yes, because I had Jesus.

The God's promise to the Israelites in Exodus 3:12 waken courage in my heart: "But I will be with you, and this shall be the sign for you, that I have sent you: when you have brought the people out of Egypt, you shall serve God on this mountain."

I am surely not Moses, and God has not called me to lead his people out of slavery in Egypt, but there are many similarities between Moses and me. After spending forty years living in Pharaoh's house then spending another forty years in Midian herding sheep, Moses was eighty when God called him to go lead the people out of slavery. He also had knowledge and supposedly some maturity, but he wasn't so sure he was qualified for the task. In fact, in this same chapter, you will read multiple instances where Moses told God the reasons he wasn't qualified to do the job.

I remember these kinds of conversations because I have had them too. I have lain awake at night in my rack thinking, "I will never make it through tomorrow." Fear of failure can stop us in our tracks, preventing us from accepting the challenge of God's call.

God's response to me in prayer is the same as he said to Moses: "I will be with you."

It was confidence course day in our training. We were faced with obstacles to overcome individually from low elements like jumping from one log to another a bit higher and further away to a high ropes course that ended with a zip line. It was my day.

I struggled to sleep the night before wondering if I was qualified to be a Marine. And on confidence course day, God showed me I was.

I didn't come in first and I didn't land every part of the course perfectly, but I jumped. Those logs that got taller and further apart were what God used to challenge me to be brave and encourage me at the same time.

This was my time to jump, the day I learned to shove fear behind me and take a risk. Leaping the gap between my limitations and the challenge before me takes courage and faith.

I climbed onto the first one and jumped with all my might to the second.

- I just kept going.

- I didn't look down.

- I didn't stop to ponder about whether I would make it or if I could do it, I just went.

- I jumped.

- Over and over again.

By finishing the training, I learned the great value of taking the risk as I make the jump to trust God for each step of the journey.

Since those early days in the Marine Corps, I have encountered many times when God called me to take a risk to reach for what seems to be impossible.

I've learned repeatedly all he asks of me is to trust him. He doesn't demand me to improve my skills, education, networking ability, etc. He just wants me to jump, to try because I trust him.

God wanted me to follow him because he called me—not because I was qualified, brilliant, or hugely capable. My courage is grounded in the knowledge that he goes with me.

Just like Moses, I face temptation to ponder the *what ifs* and the things that could happen. But God offers us the freedom to jump, to take risks, because he has already gone before and he certainly goes with us.

How to Jump and Take a Risk:

1. **Listen to Jesus.** If we don't know what he's asking, we don't know what to do. He's asking something of all of us.

2. **Remember** that we are NOT qualified (ever), but HE is (always).

3. **Be willing to try as you trust in his presence.** Trusting in Christ builds courage and confidence. He has always been there. This time will be no different.

4. **Expect amazing things to happen.** Watch for the wonder of what Christ does in and through us. It will be awesome!

Is God asking you to do something that seems too big, too hard, or too whatever? Do it. Believe God is with you and jump. Trust him.

Verses to Consider

Have I not commanded you? Be strong and courageous. Do not be frightened, and do not be dismayed, for the LORD your God is with you wherever you go. (Joshua 1:9)

Do not be in dread or afraid of them. The LORD your God who goes before you will himself fight for you, just as he did for you in Egypt before your eyes, and in the wilderness, where you have seen how the LORD your God carried you, as a man carries his son, all the way that you went until you came to this place. (Deuteronomy 1:29-31)

Trust in the LORD with all your heart, and do not lean on your own understanding. In all your ways acknowledge him, and he will make straight your paths. (Proverbs 3:5-6)

Prayer

Lord, make me BRAVE to take the risk to try new things and leap new hurdles. When I feel unqualified, incapable, overwhelmed, help me to remember that it's not about me. I put my faith in an all-powerful God who goes before and with me. Amen.

28

FREE TO BE GRATEFUL IN HARDSHIP

by Sarah McKinney

Freedom living is difficult in the face of chronic illness. Hope and courage don't come without a fight in some situations. About 3 years ago, our family changed. I changed. The diagnosis caught each of us a bit off guard. We had our rhythm and we liked it that way. Well…sort of.

You see, we *knew* she was sick…really sick. But even as my daughter's symptoms worsened, the right doctors, the right tests, or the right answers just wouldn't line up. We waited…and waited some more. And in that waiting, we learned to survive. When you don't know what to do, you just do the best you can, right? That's where we lived…clinging tooth and nail to our *ok*.

Now, let me say that typically I have had pretty decent luck with military doctors, and I have been grateful for them along the way. However, after a rapid series of moves, our healthcare continuity fell of the map. As my daughter was getting progressively worse, I was desperate for a lifeline. I couldn't see the Lord in all the *hard* and all the unknowns.

The disciples found themselves in a similar place. As Jesus prepared them for a challenging road ahead, he knew they would need to make a choice. They could choose to lean in to the world, the hardship, and ultimately fear what they had no control over. The other option opened the door to pursue life and freedom. And as they struggled with those choices, Jesus beckoned them with these words: "Peace I leave with you; my peace I give you. I do not give to you as the world gives. Do not let your hearts be troubled and do not be afraid" (John 14:27 NIV).

Jesus never tries to make this broken life work. He is fully aware that earth is not our home. Jesus reaches to the heart and

123

challenges the feelings that can either paralyze us or set us free. Instead of fear, he offers peace. Instead of worry and anxiety, he extends an inexhaustible grace.

And as we accept all that Jesus offers, we discover *freedom*.

He didn't promise that the diagnosis would be the one you or I want. Believe me, I sure wish he did. He doesn't even promise that we will be healed…at least not this side of heaven. But the truth is, at the end of this very day, you might still be suffering.

You might still be hoping, begging God to move and restore what is broken. That's ok. Go ahead and put that in his tender hands. But don't confuse his timing for deliverance with your obedience in gratitude. Yes, friends, even in chronic illness we can choose a grateful life. The life right where we are is indeed beautiful if we choose to see the beauty he offers. And if we choose to see it, we surely won't miss it.

The first intentional step toward freedom is to deliberately notice the good. Train your eyes to see that not everything is broken, not everything is a problem. When the hard and the broken clamors and complains, the good is often easy to miss. Decide to look for it. And when you notice it, capture it. Write it down.

The walk of faith may feel like two steps forward and one step back, but don't dwell on the difficulty. Celebrate the victories, even if it's small—progress is hard-won and well deserved. Gratitude is a worthy and empowering practice to cultivate.

I confess, it took time to discipline myself to notice the good in the midst of all the difficulty. But I can testify that as I did, joy got a whole lot easier to capture, too. Some days are still pretty challenging, but *hard* is not where I live anymore. Not necessarily because my circumstances have changed a whole lot, but because my heart has found freedom in spite of pain.

How to Be Grateful in the Midst of Hardship:

1. **Write it** - Make it a goal to capture daily God's goodness and tender mercies. Write them down. Challenge the rest of your family to contribute how they are seeing his goodness, too. I promise you, it's always there. Become experts at capturing the good!

2. **Display it** – Put your list somewhere where you and your family will see it every single day.

3. **Read it** – again. Often and regularly, read the list out loud to yourself and to your family. Trust me, reciting the good provisions of the Lord is biblical and is all over the old and new testament (because God knows how forgetful we can be).

I'm happy to report that my daughter is doing much better now! We are beyond grateful for progress and growth. Our lives are different now, for sure. I can testify that making this list has changed, not just our perspective, but our hearts, as well. We still navigate the ups and downs that chronic illness throws our way, but joy and hope have definitely returned to our sacred spaces…and that's always a good thing.

Verses to Consider

Restore to me the joy of your salvation and grant me a willing spirit, to sustain me. (Psalm 51:12)

I remain confident of this: I will see the goodness of the Lord in the land of the living. Wait for the Lord; be strong and take heart and wait for the Lord. (Psalm 27:13-14)

Prayer

Lord, thank you for peace that passes understanding. Open my eyes to notice the bounty of grace you give for each moment, no matter how hard. Help me to trust you beyond where I can see. Amen.

29

FREE TO REJOICE

by Kori Yates

I am an optimist.

In "spiritual talk," one of my spiritual gifts is exhortation. I have thought for years that I should get some pompoms. Not because I would necessarily look cute in the cheerleader outfit, but because I do love to cheer people on. I love to see what God is doing and I always anticipate his next big thing. It can be a challenge at times (my husband some days asks me to join him in reality), but, oh my, the blessings it can bring.

In this crazy military world where I live, optimism is hugely beneficial.

- Waiting for orders 'til the very last minute? I'll say, "maybe God will take us somewhere we've always wanted to go!"

- Experiencing a deployment? I think, "this is a great chance for us both to grow in our walk with the Lord!"

- Wondering what will come next after the military I imagine, "God is going to use us in some really cool ways!"

Through the waiting, walking, and wondering, I am look for the good. Just like everyone else, I have my challenging days, but I am thankful that I usually bounce back to optimism in no time. It's just life in my happily ever after.

Positivity is good, but optimism and rejoicing are not the same.

Optimistic as defined by Dictionary.com is "disposed to take a favorable view of events or conditions and to expect the most favorable outcome."[7] To rejoice on the other hand is "to be glad; take delight (often followed by in)."[8] Did you notice that the first is used as an adjective but the second is a verb? Rejoice is a verb. It means I am "doing" something.

In the Bible the Lord calls me to rejoice, not to be optimistic.

What exactly does it look like to follow the instructions of Paul: "Rejoice in the Lord always; again I will say, rejoice" (Philippians 4:4).

In his letter to the Philippians, Paul was adamant about rejoicing. Crazy, but Paul actually wrote these words from a prison cell in Rome. This wasn't an optimistic man who knew he would be delivered from captivity. Paul chose to rejoice, to be glad, in the Lord. His joy had nothing to do with circumstance or situation, but everything to do with his Savior.

The question then comes: HOW do we rejoice? What does that actually look like in real life where I live? In my pondering and learning, I realize rejoicing comes from remembering.

How to Rejoice:

1. **Remember who he is:** We serve a mighty and powerful God beyond all of our comprehension. A God so vast and big that we cannot even imagine and yet loves us so much to manage the details of our lives, this is who God is. He was that way yesterday. He is that way today. And tomorrow he will be the same.

---

[7] https://www.dictionary.com/browse/optimism?s=t
[8] https://www.dictionary.com/browse/rejoice?s=t

2. **Remember what he has done:** He has done amazing things in all of our lives, but sometimes we simply forget. If we take the time to go back and remember, we will surely rejoice in the awesome things he has already accomplished in, through, and around us.

3. **Remember what he said:** God has given us promises of his faithfulness, of his love, of his mercy, of his power, and of his plan. He has promised us much, and he never fails to deliver.

Remembering the faithfulness of God strengthens us to live in freedom. One thing that really helps me remember is to write it down in my journal or go back and read my journal from seasons past. Seeing it written down helps me to acknowledge who he is and what he has done. Be intentional to write down how you see God working in your life.

Rejoicing is a choice. It is something we can do regardless of circumstance or situation. Choose well today.

Verses to Consider

He is the image of the invisible God, the firstborn of all creation. For by him all things were created, in heaven and on earth, visible and invisible, whether thrones or dominions or rulers or authorities—all things were created through him and for him. And he is before all things, and in him all things hold together. And he is the head of the body, the church. He is the beginning, the firstborn from the dead, that in everything he might be preeminent. For in him all the fullness of God was pleased to dwell, and through him to reconcile to himself all things, whether on earth or in heaven, making peace by the blood of his cross. (Colossians 1:15-20)

Bless the LORD, *O my soul, and forget not all his benefits,
who forgives all your iniquity, who heals all your diseases,
who redeems your life from the pit, who crowns you with steadfast
love and mercy, who satisfies you with good so that your youth is
renewed like the eagle's.* (Psalm 103:2-5)

*I have stored up your word in my heart, that I might not sin
against you.* (Psalm 119:1)

Prayer

*Lord, help me to rejoice as I remember who you are, what you
have done, and the promises of Scripture. Empower me with
boldness to rejoice in your faithful presence regardless of what is
happening in my life today. Give me courage to choose joy that
draws others to you. Amen.*

30

FREE TO PURSUE EXCELLENCE

by Liz Giertz

When I was a soldier I focused on making sure everyone knew I was good at my job.

- I created the brief.
- I scored high marks on the test.
- I wrote the plan.
- I developed the solution.
- I earned the reward.

I was all about *me* and making sure everybody else knew how competent I was. To some extent, military culture makes some degree of self-promotion necessary, because if you don't take credit for your accomplishments, you can bet somebody else will gladly claim the pat on the back.

Over the years, I've learned to walk closer with the Lord and my pride has been a target for many of God's lessons. Though I'm no longer serving on active duty, I see how pride held me hostage to self-promotion early in my career.

It's true that pride can foster a me-centric mentality, but sometimes the pride pendulum swings too far to the other side.

It doesn't matter whether you are an active duty member, single or married, a stay-at-home-mom, a working mom, a professional, or an empty nester—recognizing our pride can be paralyzing for Christians who are taught to be humble. I've seen too many women shrink, fade, minimize, or deflect when faced with praise for work well done. I've even watched a few women avoid taking high profile positions because they didn't want to appear prideful.

But humility doesn't mean hiding. Quite the contrary. We were made to shine!

Nor do people light a lamp and put it under a basket, but on a stand, and it gives light to all in the house. In the same way, let your light shine before others, so that they may see your good works and give glory to your Father who is in heaven. (Matthew 5:15-16 ESV)

Jesus was perfect (which none of us will ever be) and without pride. He performed miracles and spoke to huge crowds. He pursued excellence in everything, understanding the purpose of his life was to reveal the glory of his Father. Our purpose is the same.

We are free to pursue excellence because the God we serve is most excellent. If we claim to be made in his image, why would we even entertain the idea of giving anything less than our best.

Pride suggests an inflated evaluation of our talents, deeming ours superior to others' abilities. Humility brokers an honest assessment of both our flaws and abilities, while seeking serve others in love. As God's Son had every right to demand his status be respected, Jesus served us to the death. Not to promote himself, but to bring glory to God the Father.

We can put aside our pride and stop hiding behind humility by understanding the purpose behind our performance. Recognize what a privilege it is that God would work through us to reveal his glory to the world.

When we replace our pride with God's purpose, we are free to pursue excellence.

How to Pursue Excellence:

1. **List** the excellent qualities God has equipped you with, thanking him for each of them. 1 Corinthians 12:4-11
2. **Lean** into Jesus with an understanding that without him we cannot do anything good or of lasting value. John 15:5
3. **Look** for ways to use your skills and abilities to serve others. Trust God to provide opportunities. Ephesians 2:10
4. **Listen** for the Lord's leading as you pray for guidance and direction. He is faithful to inspire you through the Holy Spirit and his Word. 2 Timothy 3:1-17.

As a writer, sharing my words creates mixed emotions at times. Sure, sometimes the fear of rejection makes me want to hide, but more often, I hold my words hostage in hopes of not seeming too self-promotional. I'm learning that if I truly want to shine for God's glory, I need to hone my gifts and share them with the world. If I hide what's best about me, I'm cheating God and all those around me desperate to know him more. Shifting my mindset from the idea of sharing what I write to one of serving others with the words God gives me transformed the way I look at pursuing excellence in my current career.

Are you hiding your gifts? Is pride holding you captive in any area of your life? Consider how pursuing excellence in one or more of these areas might fulfill God's purpose for your life. Look for people who share similar skills or abilities. Start or join a group and encourage one another to pursue excellence as you commit to shining together for God's glory!

Verses to Consider

For we are his workmanship, created in Christ Jesus for good works, which God prepared beforehand, that we should walk in them. (Ephesians 2:10)

I praise you, for I am fearfully and wonderfully made. Wonderful are your works; my soul knows it very well. (Psalm 139:14)

Whatever your hand finds to do, do it with your might, for there is no work or thought or knowledge or wisdom in Sheol, to which you are going. (Ecclesiastes 9:10)

Prayer

Lord, thank you for creating me in your excellent image. Show me your purpose for my gifts so that I can be free to pursue excellence for your glory. Amen.

31
FREE TO SAY NO

by Kori Yates

Saying "no" is one of my greatest challenges. I am a doer by nature. I take James' words to heart when he says, "But be doers of the word, and not hearers only, deceiving yourselves" (James 1:22). Somehow, I miss the few verses later when he talks about bridling your tongue.

Truthfully, though, saying no is SO HARD! I tell people all the time that I married my husband so he could hold my hand down when people call for volunteers.

In this military world, I think it's even harder. There are more opportunities than people and it is the nature of our culture to "sign up." From meals to school helpers and MWR to USO, opportunities abound. All good ones, mind you.

There are significant needs and finding the things I *should* do instead of just the things I *could* do can take some work. People mention a need here or there and my first thought is always, "That wouldn't be too hard." All those little *easy tasks* I sign up for, though, end up overwhelming my life.

Good things, but not always God things.

I am still learning the lessons of choosing wisely, remembering I am not responsible for the whole world. I have to take time to recognize that God has created me to do something but not to do everything.

But seek first the kingdom of God and his righteousness, and all these things will be added to you. (Matthew 6:33)

Saying "no" isn't about walking away from the right things. It's about choosing Christ over all, about seeking the Lord first— "seeking first his kingdom."

It's interesting that this verse comes at the end of a series of verses that talk about not being anxious or worried about anything.

Choosing to seek God's Kingdom means saying no to things not of him or not what he's called us to do, and doing so also helps us step away from worry and anxiousness.

Did you catch that? Saying no provides relief from worry and anxiety. As we learn to say no, we discover the rest and peace Jesus graciously promises to all believers. As we learn to use our freedom in Christ to say no to the things of the world, we'll be better able to discern where we are called to say "yes." The Lord has a perfect plan for each of our lives and longs to show us.

How to Be Free to Say No:

1. **Relationship**: It's hard to know what the Lord would have us do if we haven't spent time with him.

2. **Wait**: When you're asked, take at least 24 hours to think, ponder, and pray about it.

3. **Accountability**: Have someone you give you honest feedback about your answer. It is important that following Jesus is important to them as well.

4. **Trust**: Trust that if the Lord hasn't called you to it and he wants it to be done, he has someone to do just that thing.

Spend time with the Lord and ask him what he would have you do and make a list of those priorities. Make sure you have an accountability partner and if you don't, this would be a good time to find one.

Verses to Consider

But be doers of the word, and not hearers only, deceiving yourselves. For if anyone is a hearer of the word and not a doer, he is like a man who looks intently at his natural face in a mirror. For he looks at himself and goes away and at once forgets what he was like. But the one who looks into the perfect law, the law of liberty, and perseveres, being no hearer who forgets but a doer who acts, he will be blessing in his doing. (James 1:22-25)

Now may the God of peace who brought again from the dead our Lord Jesus, the great Shepherd of the sheep, by the blood of the eternal covenant, equip you with everything good that you may do his will, working in us that which is pleasing in his sight, through Jesus Christ, to whom be glory forever and ever. Amen. (Hebrews 13:20-21)

Prayer

Lord, show me what you would have me do and help me have the courage to do only those things. Amen

32

FREE TO BE ME

by Claudia Duff

My military ID card expired!

An expired ID card will strike fear in the heart of everyone associated with the military–dependent, active duty, retiree, or reservist. Your ID card is EVERYTHING. You need that card to get food, health care, gas, or access to the pool. It's second nature to show that card everywhere you go, even inadvertently to the Walmart greeter. (You know you have done it at least once in your life!)

I learned my ID card was expired from the gate guard, which was not a great situation. So, my husband got up before the crack of dawn and drove me three hours north to get a new one. I was a wreck until I got that hot little piece of plastic in my hands. I didn't even care that I had "hat hair," making my photo resemble a mug shot. Doesn't matter, I get to buy food and gas on military installations again.

I felt like a no one, a non-person, because of that brown card with the expired date. I realized I felt like I was EXPIRED. End of story. That was the sum of who I was as a person.

Some days those feelings extend beyond just an expired military ID card. I feel expired and discounted in my soul.

Lately, it's been a struggle to beat back those feelings of *just not enough*. Not enough time to complete my intended tasks. Not enough patience for the people in my everyday life. Not enough joy for the journey. Not enough faith to stand firm. Just flat out *not enough* of me for my life. It's unsettling and scary all at once.

But then I must remember who I am. I am a believer in Christ. I am redeemed and I am greatly loved by a great God. I know this because his Word declares it: "Behold, I have engraved you on the palms of my hands" (Isaiah 49:16 ESV).

The God of the universe knew my name before was born. The Creator has always known me. Never forgotten or set aside, I am forever, eternally engraved on the palms of his hands. There are marks that bear my name. I am unforgettable.

In order to be free to be me, I had to become intentional about remembering my identity in Christ. I could no longer just say the words, I had to begin to live the words of faith. Trust me, there is a difference.

I confess the words of Christ, read my Bible, journal the words and speak them aloud. Either to myself or to a *battle buddy*. Lately my son Josiah has been that *battle buddy*. He calls his Momma at least once a week, just to check on me, and we talk. We don't talk about much, but we always chat about our faith. He encourages me and I encourage him, and by the time we hang up, we are both convinced we are indeed saved by grace.

We will never do this walk of faith completely without failure, but we sure can give it our all. We can walk by faith, free in our identity in Christ.

How to Be Free to Be Me:

1. **Spend time with God every day in prayer.** Write these prayers down on 3×5 cards and tuck them in your Bible. I sometimes write out the verses that I want to pray over parts of my life, such as finances, marriage, children, careers and such.

2. **Worship the Lord through music.** Make a playlist on Pandora, Spotify, iTunes, YouTube, etc. YouTube is

my jam for this season. I have a few playlists based on what I am doing at the time. Blast it and remember whose you are!

3. **Share it!** Tell someone often about the God of redemption. Make a point to call a friend, family member, whoever, and share the gospel. It is indeed the Good News!

Verses to Consider

Fear not, for I have redeemed you; I have called you by name, you are mine. (Isaiah 43:1)

Christ Jesus came into the world to save sinners, of whom I am the foremost. (1 Timothy 1:15)

Therefore, if anyone is in Christ, he is a new creation. The old has passed away; behold, the new has come. (2 Corinthians 5:17 ESV)

Prayer

Lord, I'm grateful for your love. Give me "strength to comprehend with all the saints what is the breadth and length and height and depth, and to know the love of Christ that surpasses knowledge, that you may be filled with all the fullness of God" (Ephesians 3:18-19). *Amen.*

33

FREE TO WAIT EXPECTANTLY

by Katye Riselli

"Hurry up and wait" is one of the phrases that best describes military life. Everything (and everyone) needs to be ready *now*, but then we wait. There's an element of waiting for all aspects of life in the military, but the most pronounced is the waiting to go. The only constant in our lives is change, so we live accordingly— poised to pack and leave as soon as someone gives the word. We're ready, but we're waiting to know exactly when and where.

A few years ago, my perspective on waiting began to shift. My husband had been assigned to a one-year, professional military education program, so we knew our time in Alabama would be brief. We anticipated news of our next assignment as early as February, so by mid-month, I began greeting my husband every evening with an expectant look, asking, "Any news yet?"

As the weeks passed, the calendar pages flipped from February to March and into April. I quit expecting good news. We'd heard too many rumors to put much credence in anything. We'd been told to expect the Pentagon. Then, maybe orders to Louisiana, but as we approached Easter, all certainty disappeared as helpful friends and mentors suggested other possible states.

The wait exhausted me. The quiet whisper in the back of my mind lured me to believe no news must mean bad news. A long wait for these orders could only mean a deployment or a remote assignment. Fear began to crowd out expectation and I steeled my heart for disappointment. If the best offense is a good defense, surely preparation for bad news would best equip me to endure the hardship tour. Dread replaced hope and I quit asking my husband if he'd heard anything.

Less than a month before the end of our assignment, I attended the women's Bible study at my church. The guest teaching our lesson was an older woman in her 90s, full of life with a huge smile. She spoke with southern sass, confidently owning her age, unapologetic about her desire to arrive in heaven, free of the aches and pains of old age.

She opened her remarks by telling us she began each day by looking out the window at the sunrise, asking the Lord, "Is this the day?" Then she would recite Psalm 118:24, "This is the day that the Lord has made; let us rejoice and be glad in it." Each day at her age is a gift, so if she woke up, she expected the Lord had a specific purpose for her in the day ahead. After all, she told us with a wink, it might be her last day so she couldn't put off today with any promise of tomorrow.

"Age rekindles your sense of expectancy," she shared. "But don't wait to be my age to live like this." As believers we live expectantly at all ages because we know Jesus. She pointed to the disciple Thomas who argued with Jesus saying, "but we don't know where you're going." Jesus' simple response speaks volumes: "I am the way, and the truth, and the life" (John 14:5-6).

In every wait or delay, we may not know where or when, but we know the way.

Through Jesus' life and death, we know the fulfillment of the promises of God to his people. Jesus proved God is trustworthy. Jesus is the visible image of the invisible God, the evidence of well-placed faith and a sure hope in any circumstance, every day.

Her words that morning struck me, shining a light deep into my heart. I couldn't ignore the stark contrast between her approach to living expectantly with confidence and my own approach of managing my expectations, preparing for disappointment. With tears streaming down my cheeks, I asked the Lord to help me trust him and to live expectantly, especially as we waited for news of our next assignment.

I'd like to tell you I went home that day and my husband arrived with orders, but he didn't. Weeks later we finally got word of our new assignment, just days before he graduated from his program. I knew beyond a shadow of a doubt that the lessons of waiting had divinely shifted my approach to life, especially in the military.

Our approach to seasons of waiting reveals our deepest beliefs.

In Christ, we are free from fear, anxiety, trepidation, doubt, and a host of other challenges that seem to threaten the foundation of our lives. We are free to trust God, compelled by his great love for us through Jesus, full of confidence because every promise in the Bible is already "Yes and amen" for those who believe (1 Corinthians 1:20)

We are free to with GREAT EXPECTATION, because no matter where we go, we stand upon a sure foundation of faith.

How to Wait Expectantly:

1) **Seek Truth:** What do you believe to be true? Do you rely upon what you can see and feel and touch in order to know it is true? Do you believe God, the giver of life, has good plans for his children? Do you believe God will provide blessing in every circumstance? When I was waiting for the military to tell us where to go, I doubted God had a good plan for me and for my family. After an amazing year with an incredible church and spiritual community, I worried about orders to a barren land where God felt far away. As I searched Scripture about God's character, I discovered truth provided a sure foundation for my heart while we waited.

2) **Speak Life**: Waiting can feel like darkness has descended. When silence threatens our confidence, we need the Light

of Life to speak truth over our circumstances. Choose a character trait of God to counter the quiet lie that whispers doubt. When waiting for orders, I rediscovered these verses that promised God's provision and protection:

I will give you every place where you set your foot, as I promised Moses. ... As I was with Moses, so I will be with you; I will never leave you nor forsake you. Have I not commanded you? Be strong and courageous. Do not be afraid; do not be discouraged, for the Lord your God will be with you wherever you go. (Joshua 1:3,5,9)

3) **Sow Faith**: The Bible tells us repeatedly God is intentional and involved the lives of his people, so we can know with confidence that every season of waiting is purposed to prepare us.

4) **See Promise:** When we live expectantly, we look for God to fulfill his promises. Seeking truth reminds us God is still at work in our lives, speaking life fills our minds and our hearts with the confidence for the journey, sowing faith lifts our eyes to watch and see promise. Let's not miss God's intentional involvement in our lives. Let's expect his provision, protection and fulfillment of every promise.

As we seek truth and speak life, we fill our minds with truth that offers deep roots, bolstering faith, and ensure we're less susceptible to fierce winds.

How we wait matters because it shapes our future.

As I felt my faith grow, I began to live with expectation. I began to look forward to our next military chapter rather than dread the proverbial shoe.

Next time you're frustrated with a waiting season, consider how the experience of God's people before Jesus' birth mirrors our own experience in seasons of waiting. God's people had seen him do great work. God had provided prophets to speak his truth, to deliver his people from bondage, to lead them in the wilderness, and to remind them of his promises. Then came 500 years of silence. Stories that passed from generation to generation began to sound like rumors. Confidence faltered. Rather than living as people of the promise, they began believing what they lived, certain only of what they could see and touch. Experience edged out expectancy in their hearts. As a result, many missed the arrival of the Messiah.

Centuries later it seems astounding to imagine people who knew God's Word could mistake the birth of Jesus for anything other than the fulfillment of his promise. Yet, how often do we do the same? How often do we mistake silence or delay for God's displeasure or departure? How often do we miss God's greatest work in our lives because we are not watching expectantly for him? Perhaps your season of waiting is the perfect time to rekindle your sense of expectancy.

Verses to Consider

Truly my soul silently waits for God; From Him comes my salvation; He is my defense; I shall not be greatly moved. ... My soul, wait silently for God alone, for my expectation is from Him. (Psalm 62:1-2, 5 NIV)

Wait on the Lord; be of good courage, and He shall strengthen your heart; wait, I say, on the Lord! (Psalm 27:14 NIV)

The LORD is good to those who wait for Him, to the soul who seeks Him. (Lamentations 3:25 NIV)

Let us hold unswervingly to the hope we profess, for He who has promised is faithful. (Hebrews 10:23 NIV)

Prayer

Lord, help me to seek your truth in my circumstances. Grow my faith in this season, bolster my confidence, and help me to dig deep roots so that I will not be swayed by fierce storms. Open my eyes, Lord, to see your mighty work in my life and the lives around me. Amen.

CONCLUSION

by Kori Yates

For freedom Christ has set us free; stand firm therefore, and do not submit again to a yoke of slavery.—Galatians 5:1

Free to be BRAVE.

You *are* free.

Free from weariness, chaos, fear, hopelessness, isolation, uncertainty, and lack.

In Christ, God has truly set us free. Free to live in relationship with him as well as enjoy the bond of community with others. Through these devotions, we have experienced God's faithfulness through Scripture and the presence of the Holy Spirit. We are reminded of his deep love, as well as the joy and hope that can only be found in him.

He will not leave you, and he will not forsake you. You are not alone. He promises every believer his indwelling Holy Spirit, providing tangible evidence of his love by sending fellow believers to come alongside us for the journey. Just as Aaron and Hur held up Moses' arms to ensure the Israelites victory in battle, our sisters in Christ do so for each of us.

Look to the right and to the left. Gaze ahead on your military journey, and glimpse over your shoulder to those following your steps—you are not alone. While the locations may change and our battles look different, these women will be the hands and feet of the Lord in your life. Link arms with them as you look for the victory you are promised.

Together, join us in discovering the power of community built upon the words of life and truth. Find the strength to thrive wherever the Lord (and the military) sends you.

Let us then, as the writer of Hebrews exhorts, "hold unswervingly to the faith which we profess" (Hebrews 10:23 NIV). May the certainty of our freedom ignite us to live in such a way that reflects our gratitude for this lavish gift.

What does gratitude look like in real life? How does thankfulness impact our lives in the military communities in which we live? In our Christian walk, gratitude determines our bold obedience to the One who set us free. Gratitude requires our words and actions proclaim the power of Almighty God.

In military life, our gratitude for our freedom is evident as we rely on his strength and resources to meet the challenges we face. We demonstrate the power of our freedom as we band together, encouraging those alongside us to stand firm in faith, freedom, and courage.

It doesn't make sense to trust and believe in Almighty God and then extend our faith only as far as we can see or understand. Mediocrity is insufficient to serve God with gratitude for what he has done for us. Our wholehearted, BRAVE lives manifest the truth of our freedom and the power of God in us.

Our freedom FROM the power of sin sets us free TO DO so much! We are free to serve, jump, soar, lead, love, hope, and believe—*because anything is possible with God!*

So, what do we do now? How do we choose BRAVE today, in our current season of life? The joy of freedom is found in daring doing the things God has called us to in this military life.

How to Stand Brave and Live Bold in Freedom:

1. **Ask God for bold faith.** Spend time with Jesus as you pursue a consistent, intentional relationship.

2. **Tighten your grip on what you believe.** Cultivate the habit of prayer. Study the Bible. Meet together with other believers. Strengthen your faith by trusting God to be faithful to his promises in his Word.

3. **Expect God to work in your life**, trusting him to give you courage to walk in freedom. Just as God did unexpected, unexplainable things in Scripture, he continues to do in our lives today. Our testimony to his work in us brings glory to him.

4. **Obey God.** Seems simple, but in the moment, obedience can be a challenge. Faith gets comfortable with uncertainty as we choose brave in the face of our unknowns. We don't always know what the next step is and we certainly don't know what the outcome will be, but we trust God's heart and rely on him to lead the way.

Whether we are active duty, guard, reserve, or veteran spouse, mother or daughter, co-worker or friend, we are all women serving God and our nation in the military community. So today, boldly live what you believe and leave a legacy of Jesus.

Together we are a powerful force. As Christian military women around the world bravely live out their freedom in Christ, , we impact the world where God places us. Our transformed lives influence our families, work places, and communities.

Together we can enjoy this military life and extend the truth of the gospel to those we meet everywhere we set our feet.

I'm in.

Are you?

Let's be brave!

APPENDIX – ADDITIONAL RESOURCES

Free from I Should
Free of Me by Sharon Hodde Miller

You are Free by Rebekah Lyons

Free from the Performance Prison
Soul Keeping: Caring for the Most Important Part of You by John Ortberg

Lifetime Guarantee: Making Your Christian Life Work and What to Do When It Doesn't by Bill Gilham

The Rest of the Gospel: When the Partial Gospel Has Worn You Out by Dan Stone and David Gregory

Holy in the Moment: Simple Ways to Love God and Enjoy Your Life by Ginger Harrington

Free from the Fear of Aging
The Gift of Years: Growing Older Gracefully by Joan Chittister

Nearing Home: Life, Faith, and Finishing Well by Billy Graham

Halftime: Moving from Success to Significance by Bob Buford

What's Next: Women Redefining Their Dreams in the Prime of Life by Rena Pederson

Spiritual Mothering: The Titus 2 Model by Susan Hunt

Free from Heart Disease
Spiritual Disciplines for the Christian Life by Donald Whitney.

Free from Conflict
The Peacemaker by Ken Sande

Keep it Shut by Karen Ehman

Caring Enough to Confront by David Augsburger

MEET THE AUTHORS

Claudia Duff is the **Assistant Events Coordinator** for *Planting Roots* and a **Staff Writer.** As a member of the PR speaking team she enjoys conducting workshops and speaking at their one-day events around the country. Claudia lives in Virginia with her retired Navy husband. Most days when she's not writing or planning a conference for PR, you can find her sitting in her sewing chair creating Grammy-made clothing for her GrandDufflings!

Liz Giertz is a **Staff Writer** for *Planting Roots* and an Army Veteran who traded her combat boots for a pink ID Card and a craft apron. She, her husband, their two boisterous boys, and one crazy shelter pup call the hills of West Virginia home, at least until her Soldier retires from active duty. She is passionate about gathering women around her craft table and encouraging them with God's Word. She also writes at lizgiertz.com and has published a pair of workbooks aimed at helping military couples reconnect after deployment, *Marriage Maintenance: Tune Up After Time Apart for Him* and *For Her.*

Kristin Goodrich, known as "KG" on the Planting Roots team, serves as the **XO** (second in command) to the Director of Planting Roots. She proudly wore a Navy uniform for eight years and has been married to her retired Air Force husband for 25 years. She is third-generation Navy and is thankful for the opportunity to raise three kids in the military community. With a tendency to laugh loudly, KG loves to read lots of books, speak in various languages, do fire mitigation, and try new activities such as ballet. She is happy to have put down roots in Colorado.

Muriel Gregory is a **Staff Writer** for *Planting Roots*, who is Christ follower, disciple maker, Bible Study teacher and lover of the Word. She is currently living in Eastern Kansas and involved in a discipleship movement for greater Kansas City. Muriel and her active duty Army husband have been married 24 years. They have three children. Connect with Muriel on Instagram @Muriel.Gregory.

Ginger Harrington, a founding member of *Planting Roots,* is the **Publishing Coordinator** for the ministry and the author of the award-winning book, *Holy in the Moment: Simple Ways to Love God and Enjoy Your Life.* An engaging speaker for military and civilian audiences, Ginger writes at www.GingerHarrington.com and PlantingRoots.net and has guest posted for *Guideposts, Lightworkers, (in)courage, The Praying Woman, For Every Mom,* and others. Ginger and her retired Marine husband have been married for 28 years and have three young adult children. Visit Ginger's website or connect with her on Instagram @GingerHarrington.

Sarah McKinney is a **Staff Writer** for *Planting Roots.* Passionate about teaching Truth through worship and the Word, **Sarah McKinney** currently serves as a weekly blog writer (Worship Wednesday) for *Planting Roots* and enjoys speaking and leading worship for various ministries and events. Sarah also served as the Planting Roots **Worship Leader** from 2014-2017. She and her beloved husband, Jeff (Army Chaplain), have been married for 23 years and have 4 amazing children.

Dr. Brenda Pace serves as Advisor on the Planting Roots staff. With with a passion to bring encouragement and hope to women, her journey has taken her from small-town beginnings in Tennessee, around the world as a military wife and back again as an author, speaker, and military ministry consultant. Her most recent book series, *Journey of a Military Wife, God's Truth for Every Step* follows the journey of multiple biblical characters and makes application to the modern-day woman. Co-authoring two books with Carol McGlothlin, Brenda's other books include *The One-Year Yellow Ribbon Devotional: Take a Stand in Prayer for Our Nation and Those Who Serve* and *Medals Above My Heart: The Rewards of Being a Military Wife*. Brenda also served eight years on the international board of *Protestant Women of the Chapel*.

Katye Riselli is a **Staff Writer** for *Planting Roots*. A known storyteller with a passion for the written word, Katye previously served as speechwriter and Deputy Communications Director for Mrs. Laura Bush. Since leaving politics, Katye uses stories to encourage women to live what they believe by digging deep roots of faith. She writes at www.katyeriselli.com about life in the military, rediscovering faith, and building community. Katye is married to Mark, and they have two daughters. They call Virginia home, but welcome family and friends wherever the Air Force sends them. When she's not writing, you'll find her chasing her girls or reading a good book. You can connect with her on Instagram @kdriselli.

Adrienne Terrebonne has served as a **Staff Writer** for *Planting Roots* and currently lives in Clarksville, TN, with her husband Peter and their three children. She is a recovering people-pleaser and lover of all things chocolate. You can find her on her blog at *blessedbeyondexhaustion.com* where she encourages women to discover Christ in the chaos of life and motherhood.

Jennifer Wake is a staff writer for *Planting Roots* and also serves as the **Administration Team Leader**. Jennifer has been a Christian for 30+ years and still learning about Christ daily. As the wife of an Army Chaplain, Jennifer has been involved in Protestant Women of the Chapel for 18+ years. Jennifer's true passion is to teach and to serve the military community.

Kori Yates is the **Director and Founder** of *Planting Roots.* Author of *Olive Drab Pom-Poms*, Kori is a popular speaker and trainer. She writes at *KoriYates.com* and *PlantingRoots.net* and has written articles for Officer's Christian Fellowship's COMMAND Magazine as well as other publications and blogs. Kori and her active duty Army husband have been married for 14 years and have two children. Visit Kori's website or connect with her on Instagram @korikyates.

ABOUT PLANTING ROOTS

They will be like a tree planted by the water that sends out its roots by the stream. It does not fear when heat comes; its leaves are always green. It has no worries in a year of drought and never fails to bear fruit. – Jeremiah 17:8 NIV

Planting Roots is a 501c3 not-for-profit organization created by military women for military women. Our goal is to empower military women to fulfill God's purpose wherever they are planted, for however long they are there. Whether we are women in uniform, military wives, female veterans or other women connected to the military, we all experience the joys and challenges of military life. We desire to build connections, planting roots of faith and friendship that provide strength to thrive in military life.

Planting Roots encourages and equips women to plant their roots deep in Jesus Christ through biblically-based resources, live events, and online community. By building connections, cultivating a deeper walk with Christ and investing in our community, Planting Roots empowers Christian military women become stronger together. Technology allows us to cultivate a global community of like-minded, faith-filled women on a mission wherever the military sends us. As Christian military women, we seek to impact our communities by doing the work God has called us to do, in the places we are planted. Together, we impact the world for Christ.

Please join our online community at *www.plantingroots.net*. Register for our email list to receive inspiration in your inbox and be sure to follow us on social media for all new resources. Find us on Facebook @MilitaryWivesandWomen; on Instagram @PlantingRoots; and on Twitter @PlantingRoots1.

We look forward to meeting you at our next live event! You can find our conference schedule on our website. By subscribing to our emails, you'll know as soon as new events are announced!

Finally please pray and consider how you may participate in the ministry of *Planting Roots*. On our website, you'll find instructions to submit a guest post for our blog at www.plantingroots.net/writers-guidelines/ or how to make a tax-deductible gift to *Planting Roots* www.plantingroots.net/support/ Every gift is stewarded to maximize every dollar and support military women worldwide.

BEYOND BRAVE
A COMPANION BIBLE STUDY

Enjoy **Beyond Brave: Faith to Stand Firm in Military Life**, the companion Bible study for this devotional. A six-week study of Galatians 5 will help you dig into the freeing truths in this key chapter in the Bible.

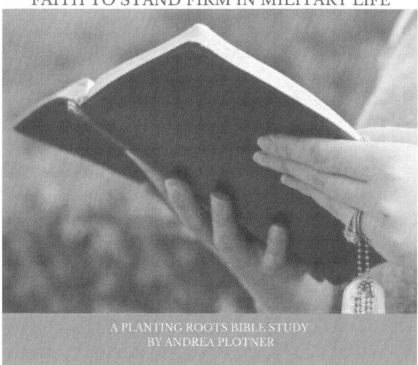

A SIX-WEEK BIBLE STUDY ON GALATIANS 5

Beyond Brave

FAITH TO STAND FIRM IN MILITARY LIFE

A PLANTING ROOTS BIBLE STUDY
BY ANDREA PLOTNER

49494066R00096

Made·in the USA
Columbia, SC
22 January 2019